SOVIET ALMANAC

WITHDRAWN

SOVIET

ALMANAC

compiled by
the editors and photographers
of Novosti Press

HARCOURT BRACE JOVANOVICH, PUBLISHERS
NEW YORK AND LONDON

Created by Media Projects Incorporated
Edited by Sara B. Stein

Printed in the United States of America
ISBN 0-15-184601-4
ISBN 0-15-683923-7 (pbk)

B C D E

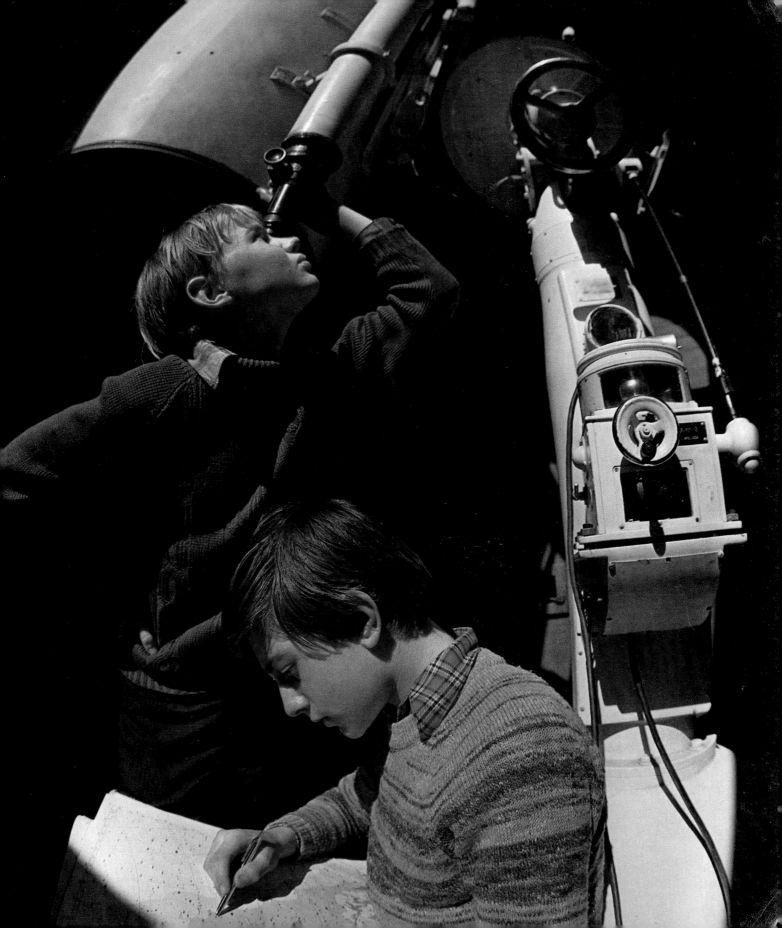

Contents

3 LIFE

1 LAND

Eleven time zones pass through the Soviet Union's territory. As the new day dawns over the Pacific coast in the east, Muscovites are sitting down to supper—and it is still yesterday. This vast country has a population of 262.5 million, made up of more than 100 ethnic groups, all speaking their own languages.

The climates and terrains in which these many and varied peoples live range through every extreme. Areas that vary in such features as relief, climate, soil and vegetation are called "natural zones." The northernmost zones are tundra (flat, boggy, covered with moss and lichen; no trees) and forest-tundra (some trees). South of these begins the taiga, or evergreen forest. Taiga, also typically flat and boggy, covers most of Siberia. The zone where the forest thins and there are natural grassy areas is known as forest-steppe. The steppe zone itself is arid grasslands, with few if any trees. More arid still is semidesert, followed by desert, complete with sand dunes.

The USSR consists of 15 equal Union Republics. The Russian Federation is the largest. Foreigners often call the entire USSR Russia, which is not correct. Although it is enormous, extending from its border with Finland in the west to the Pacific coast in the east, and including Siberia, the Soviet Far East and Far North, the Russian Federation shares equally in the national government with the other 14 Union Republics. Russians account for four-fifths of the population of the Russian Federation and altogether for 52 percent of the USSR population.

To the west of the Russian Federation along the Baltic Sea lie the 3 Baltic republics: Latvia, Estonia and Lithuania; and to the southwest, Byelorussia, the Ukraine and Moldavia. Along the Soviet Union's southern border, between the Black Sea and the Caspian, are the Caucasian republics of Georgia, Armenia and Azerbaidzhan. Also to the south, between the Caspian Sea and the border with China, lie the Central Asian republics: Turkmenia, Tadzhikistan, Uzbekistan, Kirgizia and Kazakhstan.

Under the Constitution the jurisdiction of the USSR, as the central government, covers questions of national significance such as the defense of its sovereignty and frontiers, the organization of defense, a uniform social and economic policy, and main directions for scientific and technological progress.

Each of the Union Republics has a constitution of its own. While this constitution conforms to the Constitution of the USSR, it takes account of each republic's specific cultural features. For example, although the legal marriage age in the Soviet Union is 18 years, a republic with a tradition of earlier marriage may make the legal age as low as 16 within its territory. Each Union Republic has the right to establish relations with foreign states, to conclude treaties, to exchange envoys and to take part in the work of international organizations (the Ukraine and Byelorussia are members of the United Nations). Union Republics determine their own territorial and administrative structures and exercise governmental authority within their borders. Political authority resides in each republic's own legislative bodies (the Union Republic Supreme Soviet and its presidium), government (Council of Ministers) and Supreme Court. Union Republic Supreme Soviets originate plans for their own economic and social development as well as their own budget and ratify their final versions before submission to the Supreme Soviet of the USSR. Administrative and management responsibilities include education, public health services, industry, agriculture, trade, natural resources and budget.

Because Union Republics may include various ethnic groups whose cultures are distinct from that of the republic as a whole, the USSR has 3 other political or administrative forms of self-government: autonomous republics, autonomous regions and autonomous areas. In all 3 forms, education and court procedures are conducted and laws are published in the native language. Government agencies are staffed with indigenous persons. The Soviet system of autonomy is designed to give each ethnic group a degree of self-determination in shaping its cultural, educational, social and economic growth.

There are 20 autonomous republics in the USSR, among them the Tatar, Yakut, Karelian and Karakalpak. They have both political and administrative rights within their own territories. As distinguished from the Union Republics, autonomous republics do not have the right to secede from the USSR or to enter into relations with foreign governments. They do, however, have their own constitutions, political rights and administrative responsibilities similar to those of the Union Republics. Decisions made by an autonomous republic must be approved by its Union Republic and must conform to the latter's laws.

Autonomous regions (autonomous oblasts), of which there are 8 in the USSR, have neither their own constitutions nor their own laws. Their indigenous populations are smaller than those of autonomous republics. However, they exercise considerable administrative authority within the rights granted to each by the Union Republic in which it lies. An autonomous oblast may be raised to the status of autonomous republic, with political as well as administrative rights. Of the 20 existing autonomous republics, 11 were originally autonomous oblasts. The USSR's 10 autonomous areas (okrugs) are all within the territory of the Russian Federation, and their administrative rights are set forth in a statute of the Russian Supreme Soviet. Though an okrug may occupy a vast territory, its population is typically very small.

People traveling to the Soviet Union from the West by road or rail usually come through Byelorussia. To its north lie the Baltic republics of Lithuania, Latvia and Estonia, and to the east the European portion of the Russian Federation. Both Byelorussia and the Russian Federation are bordered on the south by the Ukraine. Each republic has its own culture and treasures its own customs and traditions. But all are linked by a common history, and much of the area is familiar to foreigners through the classics of Russian literature.

Yet old books will not be of much use to tourists in these parts today; those who have formed images of Old Russia from the novels of Tolstoy or Turgenev have surprises in store for them. Much has charged beyond recognition in the years since the October Socialist Revolution of 1917. Where once the traveler saw small holdings farmed by peasants in belted blouses following wooden plows, there are now vast fields cultivated by tractors and harvested by combines.

The villages look different. Older local folk may still remember them as they were—the landowner's mansion set in parkland on the high bank of a lake or river, an avenue of poplars or oaks leading to an old-fashioned house with columns. At the farm offices behind the house at harvest time there might be a crowd of peasants hoping to be hired as temporary laborers. A row of thatch-roofed houses was strung out along the dusty road, and beside the village well rose the long pole used for dipping buckets of water. The cottages, sinking into the ground from old age, were usually lopsided, their window panes broken and stuffed with sackcloth against the wind. Inside, these oldtimers remember, were bunks bedded with straw and rags, and on the table a pot of meatless stew, a crust of brown bread.

Little remains today to remind one of those days. If it has not been pulled down, the mansion with columns has most likely been converted into a village hospital or school. The original farm buildings are now used for storing and repairing the collective farm's machinery. Comfortable new cottages with tin or tiled roofs line the newly paved road. In a large building flying a red flag are the offices of the collective farm or of the municipal authorities: their soviet, or local council. Nearby is a recreation club, as well as shops and newspaper kiosks.

Inside the cottages the traveler finds modern furniture, books on the shelves, a TV in the corner and pretty curtains. Country folk now lead a different life and have new jobs as drivers, mechanics, electricians, plumbers and librarians. There has been a swift closing of the gap between the level of education received in town and country. The communities here used to be small and quiet places with timber houses, churches of stone and market centers. Grass grew between the cobblestones in the streets. In Soviet times, plants and factories have sprung up, buildings of glass and concrete have risen and here and there building cranes rise on the horizon.

View of the Suzdal Kremlin

7

Along the western border

The population of these several republics is of varied ethnic origin and some speak quite dissimilar languages. The Byelorussians, Ukrainians and Russians are all Slavic people whose languages are closely related. Estonians are ethnically akin to Finns and the two peoples, although their languages differ, can understand each other. Both the Latvians and the Lithuanians are of separate ethnic descent and each has a unique language.

In ancient times there was already brisk trade between the Baltic peoples and the neighboring areas of Russia, Byelorussia and the Ukraine, and the region became a crossroads of trade routes from Scandinavia to the Orient. Though local alliances were formed to repel foes invading from the west, some of the lands of the Slav and Baltic peoples were long occupied by Poland, Denmark and Sweden. Particularly aggressive were the Teutonic Knights, until they were routed in 1410 by a joint force of Lithuanians, Russians, Byelorussians and Poles. The Ukraine, originally part of the Russian state but later occupied by the Poles and Turks, was rejoined with Russia in the 17th century. In the 18th century all the Baltic region and Byelorussia were united with the Russian Empire as well.

Up to the time of the 1917 October Revolution, the basis of the economy throughout Old Russia was agriculture. Although the people worked hard, primitive methods kept agricultural standards low. Industry was marginal. There were in 1913 only 55,000 industrial workers (out of a population of 6.9 million) in Byelorussia, for example. The exceptions were Latvia and the Ukraine, both highly developed industrial regions in the Russian Empire. Today each republic contributes to the USSR the products it is best able to supply. Where raw materials are not abundant, as in the western portion of the Russian Federation and in the Baltic republics, industry is based on products requiring great skill and highly qualified workers, such as electronics and home appliances, precision instruments and machine tools. Where there are forests, both in the Baltic republics and in Byelorussia, timber processing is well developed. In the Ukraine, major deposits of coal and iron ore have guided the growth of that republic's industries.

Agriculture too has developed in different ways, depending, not only on what nature has to offer, but also on the special and traditional skills the inhabitants of each republic bring to collective farming. Livestock farming predominates in the Baltic republics, where relatively infertile soil dictates the use of land for grazing rather than crops. Although the local farmers have long been noted for their industriousness and ability to raise tolerable harvests from the meager soil, still they have made their greatest contribution to the Soviet economy in meat and dairy products. Fishing, both locally in the Baltic Sea and out in the Atlantic, is of major importance.

The Byelorussians, in contrast, and the Ukrainians are noted for their grain and vegetable crops. In summer, the rich black earth over much of the Ukraine is golden with wheat. The Ukraine includes some of the most fertile soil in the

(Opposite page, left) Before the October Revolution peasants tilled the land with wooden plows. Villages were accessible only by dirt road. Cloth was homespun, shoes homemade and all luxuries were beyond the means of rural families.

(Opposite page, right) Today, although some sturdy log houses still stand, villages are reached by paved roads and the typical rural family can afford good clothes, modern appliances and perhaps a car. With mechanization, farmers also have more time to enjoy their new way of life.

Soviet Union. Soil in European Russia is far less fertile, and crops can be dissappointing, especially when weather disasters—short summers, cold springs or rainy harvest seasons—ruin the farmers' work. In the past 20 years there have been considerable expansion and improvement of agriculture, but harvest, milk and meat yields from the area as a whole could be improved further.

Because the history of these republics goes back so far, lovers of old architecture will find many of the cities of particular interest. Throughout Talinn, capital of Estonia, are fortress walls, old Gothic churches and ancient buildings. The Lithuanian capital, Vilnius, has a well-preserved 14th-century castle towering above it. The Latvian capital, Riga, has a strong air of antiquity within the city center where medieval buildings and narrow streets have been preserved. Moscow's Kremlin and Leningrad's palaces in the Russian Federation are world-famous, and so is Kiev, "Mother of Russian Towns" and capital not only of modern Ukraine but also of ancient Kievan Rus.

Only Minsk, the old capital of Byelorussia, is a young city. It has no ancient monuments or fortifications, no reminders of Old Russia. It was crushed to the ground by the Nazis during the Second World War. But the people raised their capital from the rubble and ashes; the Minsk of today is much more beautiful than the old city that was destroyed. Minsk now has broad streets, many trees, and bright, tall blocks of flats.

9

The population of Moscow, capital of the Soviet Union, is approximately 8 million and is growing by 100,000 people a year. To keep pace with its population, the city too must grow. Every day 500 Moscow families move into new apartments, and every year 60 new kindergartens and 21 schools are opened. Implementing the 1976–1980 5-Year Plan, Moscow spent a total of 17.7 billion rubles for reconstructing industry, developing housing, building cultural and community facilities, improving transit, creating parks and protecting the environment. Olympic construction was provided for in the city budget by making certain modifications in Moscow's long-term plans. For example, the Severny Luch (Northern Ray) thoroughfare linking the center of the city with its northern outskirts was originally to have been completed by 1990. Since it passes the area of Mir Prospekt where Europe's largest indoor stadium was built for the games, the Northern Ray was completed 10 years ahead of schedule.

Where does Moscow get its money? Moscow's revenues, like those of other large cities, are made up of monies received directly by allocation from the profits of local industry and indirectly through central-government allocation. Central-government allocations to the city are also largely derived from local sources: a portion of industrial levies, though paid to the central government, is allocated back to Moscow; and the same is true of personal levies on Moscow residents. Should both direct and indirect allocation be insufficient additional monies can be provided from the republic's budget and/or from the USSR national budget.

Up to 60 percent of Moscow's revenues is derived from the profits from its

Moscow, capital city

local industry and numerous other sectors of its economy such as car repair shops and cinemas. Industrial levies account for about one-third of Moscow's revenues. Levies imposed on the population, including those paid by car owners and by persons engaged in private practice (including dentists, tailors, shoemakers and typists) make up only 6.4 percent of the city's revenues.

To arrive at a budget, the Budget Committee of the Moscow City Soviet first establishes the city's financial needs for the forthcoming year. On the basis of past profits and profit planned for the coming year, it then figures how great an allotment to request directly from local Moscow industry and what indirect allotments are to be expected. The final budget of the committee is a realistic plan that balances available funds against the needs of local industry (allotments go in both directions, and cities often assist their industries), the physical and cultural needs of the city, and the social good of its inhabitants. The Moscow City Soviet, after approving the budget, submits it to the Supreme Soviet of the Russian Federation, which in turn submits it to the Supreme Soviet of the USSR.

Here it is important to understand that all budgets are coordinated with one another, so that, depending on both the Russian Federation's plans for its own republic and the USSR's plans for the nation as a whole, either or both Supreme Soviets may modify Moscow's budget. The city may be allocated more money than requested, or less, or the final budget may stipulate the same total amount to be spent in somewhat different ways.

The city's housing program—about 110,000 new apartments each year—accounts for about 33 percent of municipal expenditures. Public health services, education and cultural activities account for about 40 percent of the city's expenditures. The rest of the city budget goes toward developing municipal transport, carrying out city improvement projects and environmental protection measures.

(Opposite page) *New construction is so typical of our rapidly growing cities that building cranes seem almost a permanent part of the city scene.* (Right) *Historic areas such as the Kremlin appear unchanged by contemporary life, but that effect has been achieved through lavish expenditure for restoration and preservation.*

11

Behind fortresslike walls, the gilded towers of the Novodevichii Convent remind Moscow citizens of their architectural heritage. To integrate such monuments with new construction, city planners pay careful attention to the scale of surrounding buildings.

(Above) *The oncologic research center of the USSR Academy of Medical Sciences is an example of contemporary architecture in the capital.* (Left) *The new Salyut hotel complex was completed in time to welcome guests to the 1980 Olympics.*

(Overleaf) *The Moscow Kremlin viewed from across the Moskva River*

13

(Above) *The Valdai uplands in Central Russia are gently rolling, and fields are interrupted by patches of woodland. (Opposite page) Landscapes in the Rostov region are typically flat, as in most of South European Russia.*

Russian countryside

The lives of Leningrad's nearly 5 million people are often disrupted by the elements. In the 276 years of its existence, the city has been flooded 245 times, most recently in 1979. The floods are caused when heavy winds from the northwest push the waters of the Gulf of Finland against the mouth of the Neva River, preventing its water from draining into the sea. Sometimes the river rises 4 meters above its normal level, and could, according to experts, rise 5 meters or even more. Under such flood conditions, 12 of the city's 21 districts would be under water.

City authorities have long been combatting this recurring natural calamity.

Drains and granite embankments have been built, and houses raised on high foundations. A storm warning is sounded several hours before the river overflows its banks. Residents have enough time to protect themselves, but of course it is not possible fully to avoid the consequences of flooding. The protective measures that have been taken so far are considered only a palliative.

A decision to construct a complex dam system to protect Leningrad from floods was taken late last year. The new installation, to be located out in the Gulf of Finland and completed by 1990, will be a series of 8-meter-high dams, each 25.4 kilometers long. The dams will not look

like a solid wall, but, rather, like a giant comb. In the gaps, 6 flood control units, each fitted with dozens of circular openings 24 meters in diameter, can be rapidly closed by shutters to block even the highest wave.

Since Leningrad is a large port, there will be 2 gates in the dam system. In fair weather they will be opened for ships to pass through, but when there is a storm warning they can be closed within 30 minutes by wheeling into place the huge tight-fitting concrete shutters.

The new dam system will also provide a new highway—a 6-lane road that will make it possible to direct traffic along a short route bypassing the city.

Leningrad, old and new

Throughout its history, Leningrad has suffered disastrous floods. (Left) Strollers keep tabs on the water level as the Neva begins to overflow its embankments. (Above) Traffic struggles hubcap-deep during a flood in the fall of 1967. (Below) Major flood levels are recorded on a stone monument.

In the future, an ambitious dam system in the bay of Finland will keep the Neva within its embankments, thus protecting famous buildings such as the Hermitage (below, right) and the Admiralty (below, left).

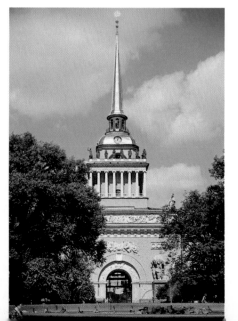

New districts have extended modern Leningrad
well beyond its former boundaries. (Above)
A residential district focuses on a memorial to
the defenders of the city during the Second
World War. (Right) Krasnoselskii district,
like most new areas, consists primarily of housing.

(Opposite page) Tall blocks of apartments are
visible in the distance beyond the Peter and
22 Paul Fortress, which dates from 1703.

Towers of the Old Town in Talinn, Estonia,
are remnants of the original walled medieval
city founded 825 years ago.

Within the Old Town of Talinn, residents go
about their daily life in ancient buildings and
along the original winding streets.

The Baltic republics of Latvia, Estonia and Lithuania have together fewer people than the city of Moscow. Yet these small lands, dense with pine forests and bordered by the sea, produce much more meat, milk and butter per capita than the average figure for the other republics of the USSR. The earnings of Estonian collective farmers specializing in dairy, pig and potato farming are above those of factory and office workers, though the opposite is true throughout most of the rest of the Soviet Union. The farmers' industry and skill are traditional, and today that experience has been translated into collectives known for their advanced automation, modern machinery, effective land management and excellent agricultural specialists.

These 3 republics are, however, by no means purely agrarian. The Baltic Sea washes more than 1,000 kilometers of a coastline that forms excellent harbors that freeze over only lightly in winter and can be used for shipping even without the help of icebreakers. The coastal peoples are experienced fishermen who go thousands of miles for their catch. Together, the 3 republics supply nearly a fifth of the USSR's fish and export fish products as well.

The hard work and persistence that have made the Latvians, Estonians and Lithuanians successful in their traditional occupations have given them equal success in modern industry. Their shipyards produce oceangoing vessels, their factories turn out heavy equipment such as turbines and railway carriages as well as

24

Baltic republics

St. Anna's Church in Vilnius, Lithuania, is one of many historic monuments restored and maintained by the city.

Chimney sweepers ply their trade on the old rooftops of Riga, Latvia, as have generations before them.

consumer products that require great diligence and skill—transistors, tape recorders, color television sets, telephones and computers.

Hundreds of thousands of people from all over the Soviet Union and foreign lands come to the Baltic Sea resorts for a rest or cure. Palanga, in Lithuania, is probably the Soviet Union's best appointed and most fashionable resort. It has dozens of sanatoria, hotels and camping sites. Its promenades are not unlike those of Ocean City, Maryland.

Tourists enjoy the Baltic lands not only for their modern resorts, but also for their ancient history. Vilnius, capital of Lithuania, was originally a walled medieval town, and few cities in the world have so many architectural monuments in so small a territory. One portion of the city is a preserve protected by the government, and each year one-tenth of the city's budget is reserved for restoration of historical buildings. Talinn, 825 years old, has also preserved much of its medieval architecture.

The Baltic republics have a rich as well as an ancient culture. The first Lithuanian book was printed in 1547, and Vilnius University celebrated its 400th anniversary in 1979. Even when the tsarist government outlawed the printing of books and school instruction, Lithuania held out in the struggle to preserve its literary and educational traditions. Many individuals in all 3 republics have chosen to continue the practice of their customary religions—Catholicism in Lithuania, Lutheranism in Estonia and Latvia. 25

A combination of fortunate location and a tradition of hard work lends the Baltic republics a distinctive character. (Opposite page) *The picturesque seacoast supports a vigorous fishing industry and also attracts tourists to its many resorts and yacht clubs.* (This page) *Inland, a modern chemical plant or a stock farm are as common these days as village windmills used to be.*

27

Byelorussia is a flat land, covered with grassy marshes and extensive forests. The Byeloveshskaya Pushcha forest contains virgin stands of centuries-old oaks. Its luxuriant water meadows are preserves for rare plants, and an animal once thought extinct—the auroch or European bison—grazes in forest clearings. Most of the swampland in Byelorussia is in the south, in the vast forested region called the Polesye. The mild climate here and the huge areas of fertile, moist soil both encourage agriculture. Yet the Polesye is rather poorly developed compared to other regions in European USSR because the numerous swamps hamper road building and the ecology of the area is difficult to manage. Hundreds of thousands of hectares of fertile land are flooded during the spring. Lands drained of excess water, however, suffer from erosion, and drainage projects threaten the ecology of nonfarm areas.

At the region's administrative center at Pinsk, the Polesye's complex problems are being tackled. Agricultural development of the region will require regulation of water drainage and the creation of a closed water supply system. The Pinsk department for land drainage has developed an anti-erosion program that includes irrigation systems, planting of forest belts and the digging of reservoirs. Dairies and stock-fattening farms are being built on the reclaimed land. As further protection for the Polesye, land improvements of any sort and also hunting, fishing, logging, hay mowing, grazing—even berry gathering—have been banned in an area of more than 60,000 hectares.

The persistence with which Byelorussia has tackled such problems is typical of this republic. In addition to producing a great deal of the Soviet Union's beef, pork, poultry, dairy products, and potatoes (6 percent of the Soviet Union's gross agricultural product) as well as quantities of flax and timber, Byelorussia is highly industrial. Its 75-ton dump trucks, tractors and motorcycles are exported to almost a hundred countries.

Byelorussia

(Opposite page) *Careful attention to the ecology of Byelorussia's extensive marsh and forest lands has allowed the republic to develop both agriculturally and industrially.*

(Right) *Heavy dump trucks are produced at the automobile factory in the capital city of Minsk* (below).

The Ukraine is a republic with diversified agriculture and advanced industry. It accounts for 20 percent of the Soviet Union's national income, and is the major supplier of coal, iron ore, steel, rolling stock, diesel locomotives and aircraft.

In the principal Ukrainian industrial centers—the Donbas coal area and the Krivoi Rog iron ore basin—9 out of 10 people live in cities. Their major towns, Donetsk and Krivoi Rog, extend vertically from the tops of their 20-story buildings to the depths of their 1,000-meter mines. The air is clean, without noticeable coal dust or the smell of sulphur, and there are trees, shrubs and flowers everywhere.

In another Ukrainian town, near a chemical plant, a beaver colony has appeared. The animals have built a dam in a stream into which the plant's purified effluents are drained. Workers have planted willows and aspen which the beavers love to nibble. Such facts show that Ukrainian industry today boasts, not only the world's biggest blast furnaces and thermal power stations, but also a successful program of environmental protection.

Ukrainian farmers are past masters at growing wheat. The latest Mironov's strains of wheat developed by Ukrainian plant breeders yield up to 10 tons of grain per hectare. Because the Ukraine has such varied geography—the Carpathian and Crimean mountain ranges, the forested lowlands of the north and the southern steppe—it is one of the most important regions in the USSR for pharmaceutical raw materials. Of the 5,000 species of plants that grow in the republic, about one-third have medicinal properties. Ukrainian scientists have developed a detailed program for the conservation and use of these herbs, including estimates of current supplies,

cultivation methods, studies of folk medicine techniques and the creation of new remedies.

Lest stressing such modern agricultural research and technology give the impression that Ukrainian traditions have disappeared, one has only to visit the village of Bolshiye Sorochintsy. There each autumn 250,000 farmers assemble for the

annual fair conducted in keeping with the rituals so brilliantly described in the last century by Gogol. The bargaining and general merrymaking are followed by a sumptuous feast in the open, where national dishes are served, many of them with the celebrated Ukrainian pork fat, plus, of course, gorilka, a strong Ukrainian vodka seasoned with pepper.

Riches of the Ukraine

(Opposite page) *Pedestrians throng Kreshchatik, Kiev's main shopping street. Kiev was once the capital of ancient Kievan Rus, and many of its fine old buildings date from that period. (Below) Tourists visit the Kievo-Pechorskaya Lavra monastery, whose frescoes (right) are among the finest examples of Russian art.*

The city of Kiev is further enhanced by the lovely Dnieper River and its handsome bridges.

(Left) *In the Donbas coal basin, a heavily industrialized area of the Ukraine, waste heaps outside Donetsk are planted with trees and gardens for the health and pleasure of residents such as coal miner Alexander Pripechenko (below).*

Donbas coal basin

Industrial regions of the Ukraine were a prime target for invading forces during the Second World War. (Right) *The Dneproges Dam, a major source of power for the coal and iron industries, was heavily damaged by bombs during the war.* (Below) *Today the rebuilt dam is part of an extensive power grid.*

(Left) *The Stalingrad tractor works, photographed in 1942, is an example of the destruction suffered by the city now known as Volgograd. (Below and opposite page) Today residents and visitors honor the memory of dead heroes and of those who lived to rebuild the city at the largest of all Soviet war memorials, on Mamayev Hill, a prehistoric barrow within the city of Volgograd.*

Twenty million Soviet citizens perished during the 1,148 days of the Great Patriotic War, as we call that period of the Second World War when the Soviet people fought the Nazi invaders. Only about half of them were servicemen. The rest were civilians who died during the shelling of cities or of starvation during the sieges of cities. Twenty-five million people were left homeless as 1,710 towns and cities and more than 700,000 villages were reduced to ruins. The invaders destroyed 32,000 factories and 62,000 kilometers of railway track. Enormous damage was done to agriculture: 98,000 collective and 1,900 state farms were wiped out. The total material losses set back the normal development of Soviet society at least 10 years.

It is no wonder, then, that the memory of the Great Patriotic War is still very much a force and presence in our lives. History and poetry about it are best sellers; many of our films concern the war. From one end of the country to another, monuments heroic in scale and style remind us of those years.

In the summer of 1942, the greatest battle of World War II began on the banks of the Volga River near Volgograd, then called Stalingrad. The Battle of Stalingrad continued with unabated intensity for over 6 months, involving at times a total of more than 2 million people on both sides. The enemy broke through to the burned-down city and fought to within yards of the Volga River. But Stalingrad won out. At its walls the Nazis lost nearly 1.5 million officers and men—more than a quarter of all their forces on the Eastern Front.

When the Battle of Stalingrad was over, the city no longer had any old monuments or masterpieces of architecture. Nazi bombs and shells had reduced Volgograd to rubble. Prime Minister Winston Churchill and President Franklin D. Roosevelt suggested leaving Volgograd in ruins, to serve, like the ruins of Carthage, as a monument to human suffering and staunchness. But it is a city revived from ashes that has become a monument to the Stalingraders' victory.

Today Volgograd stretches like a ribbon for almost 50 miles along the west bank of the Volga. High above it stands the Soviet Union's largest war monument, and in the city war museum is kept a scroll presented to Stalingrad on behalf of the people of the United States by President Roosevelt "to commemorate our admiration for its gallant defenders whose courage, fortitude and devotion during the siege . . . will inspire forever the hearts of all free people. Their glorious victory stemmed the tide of invasion and marked the turning point in the war of the Allied Nations against the forces of aggression."

Monument to courage

Peace descends over the Volga River as night falls, but during the day it is bustling with activity. (Opposite page) Most of the traffic is freight, but river boats carry passengers on outings during the summer. (Right) Small pleasure craft find anchor at a marina on the Volga embankment at Kuibyshev.

(Overleaf) The Volga River as it flows through wooded countryside

Scenes of the Volga

Leaving the capricious weather of the northwest lands of the Soviet Union, one enters the gentler climate of the south. From the farmlands of Moldavia in the southwest corner of the Soviet Union, along the coastal areas of the southern Ukraine and Russia, across the fertile plain that stretches north of the Caucasus, and down through Georgia's maritime plain, warm sea breezes create a very pleasant climate. The mountain republics of Armenia and Azerbaidzhan and the mountainous portion of Georgia are shielded from the moist sea air and so have hotter summers and harsher winters.

People are drawn to the southwest because of its unusual variety of geography and history. Lush farmland gives way to beautiful beaches, teeming resorts or rugged mountains. Along the coast, the scenery and vegetation change every 70 to 100 kilometers. The great variety of southern flora may be seen at leisure within the space of 2 or 3 hours by strolling along the avenues of the Nikitsky Botanical Gardens, founded in the Crimea during the last century. The climate here is such that even the plants of southern Italy, Greece, Algeria, Spain and the Near East can be displayed. The Nikitsky Botanical Gardens possess, for instance, the biggest grove of cedars of Lebanon outside Lebanon itself.

For lovers of antiquity, there are sites of ancient Greek cities, towns and burial mounds of Scythians and Sarmatians, and extensive archaeological collections exhibited in regional museums. Because of the great diversity of both history and nature, travelers throughout the southwest will find each town has its own unique landscape, architecture, customs and cuisine.

Most newcomers are particularly attracted to the southern areas of the Ukraine and Russia, either because they wish to settle permanently in this rich farming and industrial area or because they wish to vacation at its famous resorts.

Up until almost the end of the 18th century the fertile southern steppe of Russia and the Ukraine was a "no man's land." On the black soil (chernozem) grass grew so tall that men on horseback could not be seen above it. The Crimean khans, incited by the Turkish Sultanate, raided the area so frequently people were afraid to settle there. It has been estimated that during the 16th and 17th centuries as many as 7 million Russians and Ukrainians were captured for the slave markets of the Crimea, Istanbul, Venice, Genoa and Cyprus—a number so large that Ukrainian and Russian slaves were a "regular commodity," the mainstay of the Crimean Khanate's economy.

The Russo-Turkish wars of the late 18th century at last ended Turkish influence in the Crimea, opening the way to rapid economic development at about the same time as the American West began its similarly dramatic period of growth.

Today the same black earth that used to grow grass to prodigious height gives very high yields of grapes, sugar beets, sunflowers, tobacco, corn and wheat; the chernozem zone is, in fact, the Soviet Union's main granary. Lining the roads for many hundreds of kilometers are also apple, cherry, apricot and pear orchards 41

The fruitful South

and fields of tomatoes and watermelons. Even far from the coasts of the Sea of Azov and the Black Sea, the formerly dry climate has been humidified in recent decades by huge artificial lakes—the Tsimlyanskoye on the Don and the Kakhovka and Kremenchug on the Dnieper River. The number of days of once-dreaded dry wind—the bane of farmers—has been halved, and now the shores of the Tsimlyanskoye reservoir are solid with vineyards. The reddish Tsimlyanskoye sparkling wine is one of the most highly regarded in the USSR.

Chairmen of collective farms and directors of state farms in these fertile areas do not face the problem of young people leaving the countryside to seek work in the towns. Incomes of country people are, as a rule, higher than earnings in town. The farming villages are so big and rich they have cinemas and leisure centers, hospitals and department stores. Larger towns are close by; it is often possible to take a trolley or trolleybus from farm to town. In fact, town and village have so merged that it is quite common to see a collective farm's block of apartments and another block built by a factory for its workers standing side by side.

Nature has endowed the South with manganese, iron and nickel as well as its good black earth. A powerful heavy industry has sprung up, serving as a magnet for manpower from other parts of the Soviet Union.

People are also drawn to the coastal regions by the beneficent climate: temperatures average only slightly below freezing in January and are about 24 degrees centigrade in July, making outdoor life pleasant all year around.

An almost continuous chain of resorts runs along the Black Sea coasts of the Ukraine, the Southern Crimea and the North Caucasus. The summer influx of holidaymakers has in recent years assumed great proportions. Each resort tends to specialize in a particular kind of rest and treatment. Sochi in the North Caucasus, with its magnificent beaches, innumerable theaters, wine cellars, and festivals of all sorts is above all a resort for fit young people who come for sport and entertainment.

From October to April, however, Sochi turns from an entertainment resort into a vast sanatorium for patients with stomach complaints and rheumatism. The hydrogen sulphate and iodine bromide mineral springs there have been famous at least since the time of the ancient Greeks, who spoke of the wonder-working Sochi waters.

Many other resorts are also famous as rest homes and sanatoria. Yalta, which Hitler dreamed of making the "principal resort of the great German Army," opened the first sanatorium for peasants suffering from tuberculosis in 1925 (it is in the former palace of the tsar's family). Another resort town, Yevpatoriya, is a center for curative mud treatment for children recuperating from polio, nervous disorders and respiratory ailments.

Treatment is also available for those on holiday. Sanatoria open supplementary dining rooms for vacationers who require special diets. In every resort there are outpatient clinics and specialized medical facilities where "unscheduled" visitors can have a full medical examination, receive massage, treatment with medicinal waters and muds, and with ionized air.

At least 20 million people come each year to a total of 9,000 sanatoria, rest homes and holiday hotels from all parts of the country: from the banks of the Yenisei River in Siberia, from the Chukosk Peninsula on the Pacific, from Moscow and Arkhangelsk, by train and boat, plane and car. Where do these 20 million visitors stay? Rest homes can accommodate 10 million during the summer season from May to September. Another 2 million use the same facilities for holidays in autumn and winter. For the remaining 8 million, there are increasing numbers of campsites, and for those who prefer to stay indoors, special bureaus find accommodation in the homes of local people.

(Above) *The Gorny sanatorium is at Yalta, a resort area first opened to the peasantry in 1925 for the treatment of tuberculosis.*

(Right) *All along the Crimean coast rugged hills rising from the Black Sea create a backdrop for sanatoria such as Miskhor, perched above the sunny beach.*

43

A fruitful land and warm climate lend gaiety to Moldavia's culture. (Above) A playful structure along the approach to Kishinev is a modern expression of the city's lively traditional architecture (opposite page, top). (Left) A farm worker admires a bountiful harvest of tobacco hung to dry. (Opposite page, bottom) A vineyard worker checks bottles of wine aging in a wine cellar.

44

Moldavia is often called the "Garden Republic." The fertile soil of its plains, its mild climate and abundant sunshine provide excellent conditions for farming, and Moldavia holds first place among Soviet Republics for intensiveness of land use.

Moldavia's predominant crop is grapes, both for the table and for wine-making. Every third bottle of dry or dessert wine produced in the USSR bears a label with a white-winged stork—the trademark of Moldavia. The grape crop is so closely associated with life that on New Year's Eve Moldavians wish one another to live and bear fruit as the vine does in autumn.

Along with grapes, Moldavia raises fruit, sugar beets, tobacco, vegetables and wheat. In recent years increasing numbers of vacationers have been coming to Moldavia. They are attracted by the good climate, the Dniester River, which is considered to be one of the cleanest rivers in Europe, and of course the wholesome fresh fruits and vegetables grown on Moldavia's farms.

Life was not always so pleasant here. In the 1930's, even nails and soap had to be imported into Moldavia. Now the republic manufactures computers and other sophisticated industrial products. A land of almost complete illiteracy in the past, Moldavia is now famous for its excellent printing plants, and more than a hundred prose writers and poets are members of the Moldavian Writers' Union.

Moldavians are also gifted singers and musicians. The Fluerash orchestra is well known throughout the Soviet Union and abroad. The republic is proud of a peasant's daughter, Maria Bieshu, now a People's Artist and winner of first prize at a Madame Butterfly contest in Japan. Maria Bieshu has performed at La Scala and New York's Metropolitan Opera. 45

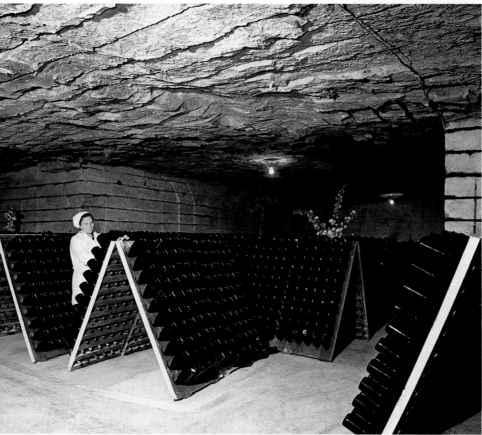

Moldavia

The Caucasus is the most versatile of resort
areas, for its snow-covered mountains afford
excellent skiing while its shores
attract swimmers and sunbathers.

Caucasus vacation

Georgia, a small, mountainous republic only half the size of the American state of Georgia, is a land of riches. In days gone by, so the legend goes, when the Argonauts came here in search of the Golden Fleece, they were amazed by the local gold jewelry. Modern Georgian artists have made the craft of metal-chasing into a monumental art. The streets and squares of many Soviet towns and also the United Nations headquarters in New York are adorned with Georgian wrought-copper murals.

Copper is just one of Georgia's riches. Many varieties of Georgian marble—blue, smoky-gray, black and red—were used centuries ago for palaces that stand to this day. Modern buildings from the Caucasus through Central Asia and Siberia—and including the Moscow Metro or subway and the Olympics stadiums—are faced with Georgian marble. Of Georgia's many other mineral resources, manganese and coal are found in the greatest quantities and serve as the basis for the republic's heavy industry.

Once an agrarian region, Georgia now produces pig iron and steel, builds electric locomotives, hydrofoil ships, airplanes, tractors and instruments for space navigation. But Georgia's traditional products have not lost their value in this space age of ours. Tobacco, citrus fruits and tea, famous throughout the country, are grown on the fertile soil of Georgia's maritime plain, the only subtropical area in the Soviet Union.

Tbilisi, the capital of Georgia, started as a health resort of sorts 25 centuries ago when shepherds founded a settlement near its hot sulphur springs. Today Tbilisi is the industrial heart of Georgia. Among its many products are musical instruments that were highly praised by the famous American pianist Van Cliburn.

(Opposite page, top) Tbilisi, capital of Georgia, is a major industrial center known especially for its musical instruments. (Opposite page, bottom) Georgia's maritime plain is the only subtropical part of the USSR, where the weather year 'round is warm enough for growing tea.

The medical profession has for years been interested in the unusual longevity among certain groups of Georgians. (Above) Scientists from the Kiev Gerontological Institute interview centenarians. Despite their advanced years, these Georgians display great vigor of mind and body.

49

Georgia

Armenia is a land of sun, mountains and dead volcanoes. Its summer heat and winter cold, its dark rocks and harsh mountains are severe. It was those sun-burnt rocks, the people's eternal curse, that brought wealth to Armenians. Rocks can be valuable—pink tufa, marble, gran-ite, basalt, even nitrate fertilizers and sili-con for transistors.

The mountains are not Armenia's only resource. The pride of the industrious Ar-menians is their fragrant peaches and sweet grapes, grown in areas where water is so precious it was once an object of worship. From the grapes are made won-derful wines and brandies that are second to none in the world.

Armenia's capital, Yerevan, was founded in 783 B.C. Matenadaran, the unique depository of ancient manu-scripts, stands at its very heart, and in Echmiadzin, not far from the capital, one can admire khachkars—ancient stone crosses—and hear a sermon delivered by Vazgen I, Catholicos of all Armenians. Armenia is also famous for its school of modern mathematics and is a recognized center of world astronomy.

Tragically Armenia of the past was a country without a people, and Armenians a people without a homeland. After the 1915 massacre, when the Young Turks slaughtered nearly 2 million Armenians, only 700,000 of them remained in what was left of their land in eastern Armenia: one-tenth of a nation on one-tenth of their homeland. That tragedy cannot be undone, but as a Soviet republic Armenia has been the motherland for its nearly 3 million Armenians, including 230,000 who, dispersed far from their homeland, were able to return.

Armenia

(Opposite page) *The pagan shrine at Garni survives from the classic era, lending a sense of timelessness to its environs.*

(Below) *Lake Sevan is one of the few bodies of water in this otherwise arid land.* (Right) *An unusually small Armenian family takes in the sights at Echmiadzin. Armenian couples ordinarily prefer large families.*

51

(Above) *Baku, once the principal oil-producing region of the Soviet Union, still supplies oil with the lowest sulphur content.* (Right) *A newer oil field, at Neftyaniye Kamny, is built on piles in the Caspian Sea.*

Traditional industries of Adzerbaidzhan include carpet weaving, still practiced by skilled weavers using handmade looms.

Medieval chroniclers called Baku, now the capital of Azerbaidzhan, "the city of fires." That poetic image was born of reality: burning jets of gas and oil flared on the ground, and the people of the area worshiped fire, built temples and made sacrifices in its honor. From time immemorial the local folk used oil to light their homes and to treat wounds and in wartime as an incendiary substance.

Baku still extracts that oil and for a long time Azerbaidzhan was the principal oil producer in the Soviet Union. It still produces oil with the lowest sulphur content, and in search of it holes deeper than 6,000 meters are drilled. The last few decades have also seen large-scale oil extraction in the open sea. In the Caspian Sea the town of Neftyaniye Kamny (Oil Rocks) has been built on steel supports 100 kilometers offshore. Its streets run on trestlework for a total of 200 kilometers, and its 5-story buildings include residences, cafeterias, clinics, schools, a greenhouse and a helicopter pad.

Today, however, Baku and other towns in Azerbaidzhan extract less oil than Tataria, Bashkiria or Western Siberia. Though its resources are likely to last many years, Azerbaidzhan is gradually changing its traditional orientation to oil. For the sake of its continued growth its government has given priority to such industries as mechanical and radio engineering, electronics and instrument-making.

Certainly the future of Azerbaidzhan is with industry, for agriculture is difficult in the republic. More than half the tilled land is saline, and crops require irrigation and considerable desalination efforts. Not easily discouraged, however, the republic today has more agronomists than Britain or Italy, and more students per 10,000 population than either Britain or France. 53

Azerbaidzhan, land of fire

East of the Caspian Sea lie the republics known together as Soviet Central Asia—Uzbekistan, Tadzhikistan, Turkmenia and Kirgizia to the south, and the southern portion of Kazakhstan. Though they occupy a vast area, one-fifth the total of the Soviet Union, these republics are united by similar natural conditions, a common historical past and economic development. The affinity of their cultures and style of domestic life took shape under powerful Islamic influence over a period of 12 centuries.

Soviet Central Asia is inhabited by the largest groups of non-Slavic peoples in the USSR: 12,400,000 Uzbeks, 6,500,000 Kazakhs, 2,800,000 Tadzhiks, 2,000,000 Turkmen and 1,600,000 Kirgiz. Karakalpaks, Dungans, Uigurs, Tatars, Jews, Koreans and representatives of virtually all the USSR's hundred or so peoples—including slightly over 9 million Russians—also live here.

Their lands are harsh. The northern part of Kazakhstan is arid steppe rather like the prairies of Kansas. Most of the rest of the region is desert or semidesert. Only in the far south is there a chain of highly fertile oases fringed by huge mountain ranges—the Pamirs, Tien Shan and Kopet Dagh. Yet Central Asia has been a center of world civilization since at least the first millennium B.C. when the state of Khorezm arose on the lower reaches of the Amu Darya River. There, where irrigation produced rich harvests despite the hot and dry climate, fortress cities were built to defend the population against the raids of nomads, and skilled craftsmen and slaves built palaces and temples.

As the route for the silk trade between China and Europe developed through Central Asia, towns along the caravan route were enriched both in goods and in knowledge. From India came techniques of cotton growing, while the Central Asians taught the art of viticulture to the Chinese. Lively ties and prosperous trade were also maintained with the Greeks and Persians.

Over a period of several centuries, Central Asia produced Avicenna, the great scientist; Ulugh Beg, an astronomer and mathematician, and Biruni, a geographer and astronomer who—500 years before Copernicus—realized that the earth rotates around the sun. Brilliant poets, including Rudaki, Omar Khayam, Saadi, Firdawsi and Alisher Navoi, lived and worked in Central Asia's cities.

The wealth of the region, however, tempted many conquerers, among them Greeks, Persians, Arabs and Mongols. It was not until late in the 14th century, when Timur Lenk or Tamerlane, an Uzbek feudal lord, managed by fire and sword to unite all the Central Asian lands that a powerful empire emerged.

Tamerlane's capital was Samarkand. There the Bibi Khanum mosque, built by Tamerlane in honor of his favorite wife, still stands, as do the refined and graceful mausoleums of Chupan Ata and Ishrat-Khona. Tamerlane's remains, undisturbed except for a brief period in 1941 when scientists examined his skull in order to reconstruct his facial features, still lie in Gur Emir, a splendid mosque with a brilliant blue dome.

Islamic architecture, Samarkand

Soviet Central Asia

After his death Tamerlane's empire disintegrated and feudal lords became involved in unending internecine strife and war. The resulting economic disruption hindered cultural advance for the next several centuries.

The annexation of Central Asia by Russia in the 19th century played a progressive role. It put an end to internecine strife; the economy began to develop at a faster rate. The first industries appeared; railroads were built; new towns and cities grew. Russian settlers brought with them the achievements of Russian and world culture, opening new vistas to the aristocracy and the educated. Of course the tsarist autocracy did not make life easier for the working people. In those days Russia was aptly described as a "prison house of nations." Central Asia was assigned the role of a colony and a source of raw materials for Russian capitalism.

The October Revolution launched the peoples of Central Asia on the road to accelerated economic, political and cultural development. In many respects it was necessary to start from scratch. In the whole of Turkmenia, there were only 1,000 industrial workers. The fields of Kirgizia were being tilled with primitive wooden implements, as they had been for a thousand years. Medieval Islamic laws, particularly repressive of women, still held sway. There were fewer than 500 qualified doctors in the whole of this vast region. But illiteracy was the worst heritage. The cultural treasures created in the past could be appreciated only by a handful of rich people and the higher clergy. Turkmenia and Kirgizia had no written languages. In Tadzhikistan and Uzbekistan, only 1 person in 200 could read and write.

At first change came slowly. Written languages had to be formulated for those who did not have them. When the Russian alphabet could not reproduce the phonetics faithfully, new letters were added. Schools were set up throughout the lands, but even so, teachers had to persuade parents to send their children to school and not to marry off their daughters at the age of 10. Doctors worked to convince people to be vaccinated against contagious diseases. Up until the 1930's, reactionary forces—including armed gangs called basmachi—attacked the schools, hospitals and clubs that began to appear soon after the Revolution. Local and Russian representatives of Soviet rule were killed at the instigation of the rich and the mullahs, the teachers or expounders of Islamic law.

But the coming of the new way of life was inevitable. In 1920 the first Central Asian university was opened in Tashkent, capital of Uzbekistan. By the time of the Second World War virtually the whole population—the old as well as the young—was literate. Today each of the republics conducts lessons in its native language and teaches its own particular curriculum of history, geography and literature. Uzbekistan alone has 45 higher-education establishments and about 200 research centers, including an institute of nuclear physics.

Whereas 40 years ago most of the population of Central Asia lived in tents or adobe homes without gas, electricity, running water or sewage facilities, the towns and settlements now have apartment houses with all modern conveniences. Nearly every family has a TV set, refrigerator, piano and telephone. The ancient culture of the Central Asian peoples is experiencing an upsurge. The Kirgiz writer Chingiz Aitmatov, the Tadzhik poet Mirzo Tursunzade and Zulfia, the Uzbek poet, are world-famous. Great Central Asian astronomers and mathematicians again study the cosmos—now at the USSR Academy of Sciences' observatory high in the mountains of Tien Shan.

Not everything has changed. Though the tradition of women wearing a veil in public died out long ago, the tradition of large families is still very much alive and keeps the Central Asian birth rate high. From 1970 to 1979 natural growth increased the population of the Central Asian republics by approximately a third, while the increase in the Russian Federation, Byelorussia and the Ukraine was only 6 percent. However, this population explosion is causing us no concern, and the people are not urged to reduce the birth rate. Nobody in the USSR sees any danger of the Slavs being "dissolved in the mass of Asians." Central Asia itself needs young forces to develop its considerable resources to an even fuller degree in the future.

(Above) *In a suburb of Tashkent, men prepare pilaff, a favorite Uzbek dish. Their hats, called tubeteikas, are customary Central Asian headgear worn also by Tadzhiks* (right) *selling their produce in a city market in Dushanbe.*

57

(Above) *Northern Kazakhstan reclaimed vast areas of virgin land during the 1950's and is now a major grain-producing region.* (Opposite page) *In Turkmenia, as in southern Kazakhstan, curly astrakhan hides from newborn karakul sheep are basic to the economy.*

(Overleaf) *The lush summer pastures of Central Asia*

Many countries are now capable of producing astrakhans—the skins of newborn karakul sheep known for their beautiful patterns of soft curls—but the birthplace of this marvel of nature is the valleys of Soviet Central Asia. Here there are over 12 million karakul sheep, almost half of the world's karakul flocks, and enough for the USSR to supply the world market with a third of its astrakhan pelts.

The modern success of this ancient breed is no accident. As part of the total development of such republics as Kazakhstan and Turkmenia, much effort has been spent extending pastureland and introducing flocks into areas where karakuls were not previously raised. This has not been easy. More than four-fifths of Turkmenia's territory is desert: the Kara Kum, an endless sea of sand rising in crests to dunes 5 stories high; the cracked clay of the takyrs, and the lifeless patches of solonets or salt flats.

Beneath the desert sands and soils, however, archaeological excavations revealed the remains of advanced ancient cultures that once thrived along a now-extinct chain of oases. Following that chain, Soviet workers built the 1,000 kilometer Kara Kum Canal, which spans the entire Turkmen Republic from the Amu Darya River to the Caspian Sea. This man-made river feeds a whole network of irrigation canals and water reservoirs around which now stretch plantations of fine-staple cotton, Turkmenia's pride. Such irrigation projects in Turkmenia also extend grazing lands and provide drinking water for sheep.

Kazakhstan stretches over a vast area—from the steppes near the Volga and Caspian shores to the northeast corner of the Mongolian People's Republic. From north to south, both the climate and the terrain change drastically, and for this reason the USSR considers only the southern part of Kazakhstan as Central Asian. Here the land is typically hot, dry and mountainous, whereas to the north, along the border with Siberia, Kazakhstan winters are very cold and windy and the countryside is flat steppe.

Reclamation of virgin and long-fallow lands began in the north of Kazakhstan in 1954. Hundreds of thousands of young people from all over the Soviet Union were attracted to the project. It was not just a question of plowing, since, once turned over, the fertile top layer of soil was vulnerable to wind erosion. Kazakh scientists had to develop special machines to cut the soil without turning it. As a result of these efforts, Kazakhstan now accounts for up to 20 percent of the Soviet Union's grain harvest. Along with the development of crops, livestock was introduced on a large scale. Among the breeds are the famous karakuls, raised primarily in the south.

59

Kazakhs and Turkmens

(Above) *Cotton, harvested by machine, is the major crop in both Uzbekistan and Tadzhikistan.* (Left) *The harvest is brought by truck to huge collection centers from which it is distributed to textile mills. Tadzhikistan is an important textile center both for cotton goods and for beautiful silk fabrics such as that woven at Fergana (opposite page, bottom).*

(Opposite page, top) *Rapid economic progress has resulted in thriving cities. The new Blue Dome Café in Tashkent reflects both prosperity and the Oriental tastes of Uzbekistan.*

In both the Uzbek and Tadzhik republics, the principal source of wealth is cotton or "white gold." Experienced cotton growers, the Tadzhiks boast the world's highest yields. Yields have been increased yearly in Uzbekistan; 1980 saw a harvest of over 6 million tons of cotton, of which 320,000 tons was an especially valuable fine-staple variety.

Progress has been difficult. Though Uzbek soil is incredibly fertile, the climate is hot and dry and there are few rivers. Today man-made canals stretch for a total of 100,000 kilometers, and reservoirs hold nearly 4 million cubic meters of water. The successful provision of water, land reclamation programs and the discovery of extensive mineral resources have helped Uzbekistan attain the best-developed industry of the Soviet Central Asian republics. It now exports cotton pickers and looms as well as raw cotton.

Tadzhikistan, like Uzbekistan, is dry and hot, but natural waterways rather than manmade ones supply needed irrigation. The republic occupies the high Tien Shan plateau and the Pamirs, including the Soviet Union's highest mountain, Communism Peak (24,600 feet). It is the mountains that provide water. Rapid streams, rising high in the realm of eternal snow, rush down the precipitous cliffs, become rivers and, cleaving narrow gorges, roll out over the valleys. There they water apricots sweeter than either American or European varieties and groves of mulberry trees on whose leaves silkworms are raised for their precious strands of silk. These streams provide irrigation for the cotton crop and also supply cheap electricity. Hydropower supplies the energy for Tadzhikstan's textile industry, which uses the fibers from cotton, silk, fine-fleece sheep and angora goats to produce its excellent fabrics.

63

Uzbeks and Tadzhiks

Central Asian architecture developed under
powerful Islamic influence. (Above) A view
over the rooftops of Bukhara. (Opposite
page) The city of Khiva. Both are in
Uzbekistan. Domes, arches and geometric
ornamentation recur in contemporary Central
Asian architecture.

Domes of Islam

Horsemen in the high mountains of Kirgizia excel in national games such as "Catch the Girl" (opposite page) and wrestling on horseback (above). Horse breeding has been the historic livelihood of Kirgizia and is practiced on a large scale today.

(Right) A modern family celebrates a festival inside a yurt, a large and comfortable dome-shaped tent traditionally made of horsehide.

Horsemen of Kirgizia

The name Siberia comes from a local expression meaning "dormant land" and, until quite recently, that is exactly what Siberia was. The severe climate, so cold that rubber tires become brittle and the moisture in a man's breath freezes to his whiskers, effectively sealed off Siberia's natural wealth. In the permafrost zone— more than two-thirds of the land—winters are so long and so cold that the soil below the surface never thaws. In summer, anyone venturing out into the taiga is attacked by swarms of tiny black flies. Only fur trappers and gold diggers used to be found in Siberia.

Not all of Siberia is icebound. Although mosses, lichens and wildflowers are the sole vegetation growing on the polar tundra, and whirling blizzards often obscure the sky for days at a time 9 months of the year, there is a strip of land along Siberia's southern edge below the taiga where the forest is not so dense or the climate so harsh. This is the forest-steppe, a land of abundance where summer is hot but not too dry, and winter, though cold, is dry and bracing. The forest-steppe is where most of Siberia's towns and cities and two-thirds of its present population are located.

Before the October Revolution, the whole of Siberia accounted in 1916 for only 2.5 percent of Russia's industrial production. Even then scientists had an idea of Siberia's natural mineral wealth, but the extraction of those minerals was insignificant. The authorities in St. Petersburg regarded Siberia solely as a source of taxes, gold and furs, all of which they received without making any investment in the area.

The first "offensive" began in the 1920's with a comprehensive geological survey followed by the establishment of a powerful center of heavy industry at Kuzbass in the Kuznetsk coal basin toward the south central part of Siberia in the 1930's. By the 1960's the Soviet Union had established an adequate economic basis to begin the large-scale development of Siberia's more northern regions. Considerable outlay per unit of output was necessary. Areas to be developed were remote from existing industrial centers and could not be reached by either road or rail. Rigorous climate, mountains, dense forest, impassable marshes and swarms of insects in summer compounded the problem.

During the first few years of construction at Tyumen in West Siberia components of drill rigs, transmission line towers and prefabricated housing were delivered by helicopters over distances as great as 800 kilometers. Since 1965, 50 billion rubles have been invested in the development of oil and gas resources in that area alone. The Tyumen oil fields have by now produced 90 billion rubles' worth of oil and gas. They have also repaid the original investment in terms of the large petrochemical industry that has developed in the area.

The growth of Siberia continues today at a rapid pace. East of Tyumen (but still only in about the middle of Siberia) a series of power plants is now nearing completion on the Yenisei and Angara rivers. Their aggregate estimated capacity

Outward to Siberia

of 50 million kilowatts will boost extensive industries already developed on the basis of cheap coal mined in the same region. The prospect for the near future is the development of regions situated even farther to the north where deposits of oil, coal, nickel, copper and tin have been discovered.

The absence of road and rail systems is still a formidable obstacle to the development of Siberia. This is why the Baikal-Amur Mainline, which will link industrial complexes from central Siberia to the Pacific Ocean, is under construction. Another railroad, this one being laid from Tobolsk in West Siberia to the world's biggest gas deposit, in Urengoi, will cross the Arctic Circle. In the winter of 1979 the first all-year navigation by icebreaker was opened between Murmansk and the mouth of the Yenisei. This route too will speed the development of the North.

It is hard to imagine, however, that the opening of Siberia will ever be easy. As resources are tapped farther north and industries based on those resources are developed, more and more communities are being built in the permafrost zone, where construction engineers encounter considerable difficulties. There are some areas where the ground, rigid in winter, heaves out huge boulders during the summer thaw. Yet during the brief but hot summer, the softened top layer of soil, like quicksand, sucks in buildings built by conventional means. Construction methods for different areas of the permafrost are worked out at the world's only Institute of Permafrost in Yakutsk in East Siberia. Today, houses are placed above reinforced concrete piles frozen into the permafrost to a depth of 7 to 15 meters, where the soil is as hard as granite. The space between the earth piles and the building provides both the insulation and the ventilation necessary to keep the ground from thawing.

The population of Siberia is now 27 million people, of whom a million are various native peoples, including the Buryats, Yakuts, Tuva, Khakassians, Evenks, Chukchi and Nentsy. Some of these minorities live in the towns and work on construction sites but most are traditionally scattered, engaged as they still are in cattle and reindeer breeding, fishing and fur hunting. The people living in the forest-steppe zone from the Ural Mountains to the Sea of Japan account for two-thirds of Siberia's population. Their average age is only 28—an indication that most of Siberia's inhabitants are newcomers. Workers earn roughly more than twice in Siberia what they would in the rest of the country. But money is not the main reason why young people go there. They are attracted by the romance of being pioneers and by an opportunity to show their worth. In Siberia a young man or woman can rapidly gain professional experience; promotion is rapid too. The directors of plants, factories and construction sites in East Siberia are on the average 14 years younger than their counterparts in European Russia.

Once, many of these young people would not have thought of staying permanently in so inhospitable a land, but today more people come to Siberia than

New cities in Siberia are planned so that buildings wrap around open spaces, thereby protecting pedestrians from the winter winds. This drawing is for the master plan of Urengoi, an oilworkers' town in western Siberia.

70

leave it. The steps taken to attract them are apparently effective, but they must also be impressed by the changes taking place: the growth and improvement of hundreds of comfortable, sophisticated new towns with cinemas, theaters, cafés and clubs; and the special benefits (a 48-day annual leave, for example) extended to all workers in Siberia.

Because of the economic, professional and moral benefits of life in Siberia, people from all parts of the Soviet Union come here to work. There are 43 percent more intermarriages here between persons from different ethnic backgrounds than in other regions, where groups tend to remain separate. However, there is still an acute manpower shortage. Our only way out is to equip Siberia's enterprises with the most up-to-date equipment. This is why the whole area has now become a huge testing ground for new machinery and for new production methods. Many of the dozens of research institutes in Siberia (they employ 4,000 scientists including 400 Doctors of Sciences—the equivalent of PhD's—and 62 Academicians, renowned members of professional societies) are tackling practical problems concerning the development of Siberia. For example, it is hoped that Siberia can become agriculturally self-sufficient. To this end, a dozen new varieties of wheat have been developed for the Asian part of Siberia, and new varieties of potatoes for beyond the Arctic Circle. Cucumbers, tomatoes and green onions are being grown in greenhouses heated either by thermal waters or conventionally with sunlight, but production is so far minuscule.

Of crucial importance in the work of the Siberian Branch of the USSR Academy of Sciences is a long-term program for Siberia's growth through the year 2000. The program proposes 30 guidelines for the rational utilization of mineral, land, forest and water reserves of the area, as well as for the development of industrial complexes scientifically planned to make the best use of local resources. Where ample coal and iron ore are combined with cheap hydropower in southern Yakutia, the industrial complex produces pig iron and steel; whereas in Bratsk a combination of hydropower and huge timber reserves has been used to develop the Soviet Union's largest pulp and paper complex. The scientists' recommendations are taken into consideration by planners and builders, and their respect for the guidelines has already proved beneficial. Specialists in the 1960's, for example, recommended building a very large power plant in the lower reaches of the Ob River. Had the ministries disregarded the scientists' strong objections to the construction, almost the entire area of what is today the Tyumen oil fields would have been submerged beneath a huge reservoir. Within the last few years, scientists objected to the destruction of vegetation that occurred when construction workers hauled building materials across permafrost areas in summer by truck and tractor. Since it takes a decade for nature to repair the damage, they suggested transporting materials in winter when snow protects the delicate surface. That suggestion is now routinely followed.

When Siberians are proud of the new community in which they live, they may compliment it by saying, "Our town is a second Novosibirsk." This is a tribute to Siberia's unofficial "capital," to its modern architecture, the high level of its scientific community, its famous theaters and its flourishing literature.

By Siberian standards, Novosibirsk is an old city, for it sprang up in 1897 at the point where the then brand-new Trans-Siberian Railway crosses the Ob River.

Since then, Novosibirsk has continued to take advantage of its situation at the intersection of the Trans-Siberian Railway and the Ob and of its proximity to the Kuznetsk coal basin and the metallurgical plants of the Urals. Today Novosibirsk is one of the most important centers of industry in the Soviet Union, providing a solid base for tapping the resources of the vast expanses of the eastern portions of Siberia. Two-thirds of its workers are engaged in engineering, geared mainly to meeting Siberia's own construction needs.

Novosibirsk, with well over a million inhabitants, is Siberia's largest city. Its main street is 18 kilometers long—one of the reasons it is known, locally at least, as "the city with the biggest everything." The city has its own university as well as a dozen other institutes of higher education, another dozen specialized secondary schools and a conservatory. The people of Novosibirsk are proud of their Academic Opera and Ballet Theater and of their Young Spectator's Theater.

Outside the city, in the virgin forest that still surrounds it, lies Akademgorodok, the "Science City" of the Siberian Branch of the USSR Academy of Sciences. There the scientists of 21 institutes direct research institutions from the Ural Mountains to the extreme eastern portions of Siberia in Sakhalin and Kamchatka.

Sophistication in Novosibirsk

(Opposite page, top) *In spite of harsh winters and an isolated location, Novosibirsk offers its residents a sophisticated city life.* (Opposite page, bottom) *The opera and ballet theater is only one of numerous cultural institutions. Novosibirsk is also a prestigious science center.* (Above) *Colleagues meet at the Institute of Nuclear Physics.* (Right) *A patient at the Institute of Pathology of Blood Circulation is prepared for open-heart surgery by lowering his body temperature with ice.*

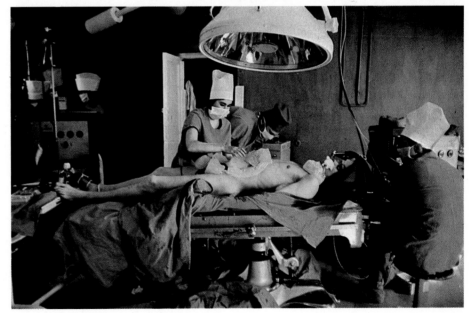

There are many navigable Siberian rivers but their uses for transport are limited. They freeze over during long winters and most of them run north/south whereas most goods must travel east/west. Nevertheless, summer on the Lena River (above, left) *is a busy season for freight. During the winter, caterpillar vehicles can travel over frozen waterways. (Opposite page, bottom) Caterpillar vehicles are kept in an inflatable garage and are even used for a wedding procession, Siberian style.*

The waterways of Siberia include Lake Baikal (this page, top) and the rivers Ob and Irtysh in western Siberia (this page, bottom).

Wilderness waterways

The trackless taiga

The taiga forests of Siberia are seemingly endless. (Opposite page, top) *In former times the only houses in the taiga were the isolated cottages of hunters and trappers. Today airplanes and helicopters transport workers of all kinds across the trackless forests to permanent new settlements.*

The indigenous peoples of Siberia, among them the Chukchi, Yukagirs, Selkups, Buryats, Evenks, Tuva, Khakassians, Eskimo and Nentsy, number altogether about a million people of 30 cultural stocks.

As in former times, the main occupation of the smaller ethnic groups is hunting and reindeer breeding. The Nentsy, reindeer breeders who live beyond the Arctic Circle, are an example of the changes that have affected our indigenous peoples since the 1930's. It used to be that whole families followed the reindeer; now only herdsmen lead a nomadic life, while their families live in permanent well-equipped settlements. From ancient times the Nentsy lived in cone-shaped tents of deer hides on a wooden pole frame. Now the typical Nenets home is a timber house. Though tents are still used when the deer migrate, they are now made of plastics and synthetic fibers. Two-way radios allow herdsmen to communicate over long distances, and sleighs, once pulled by reindeer, are being replaced by motor-driven sleighs that have a ski in front and a caterpillar track in the rear. The Far North Institute of Agriculture and other research centers in Siberia can reach even the most remote herds by helicopter. The services they offer range from the removal of gadfly larvae and other blood-sucking insects from the reindeers' coats to acquainting herdsmen with modern livestock breeding methods.

To help the Nentsy switch over to a settled life, communities have been set up in which Nenets children live and study in boarding schools for 11 years at state expense. During that period they become accustomed to new ways, and on leaving school many go on to study at higher educational institutions in such cities as Arkhangelsk, Leningrad or Moscow.

Many Nentsy and other Siberian peoples now work in oil fields or gold fields as engineers and construction workers, or they may be teachers or doctors. Particular importance, however, is attached to developing traditional occupations, for the culture of the indigenous peoples of Siberia is an inseparable part of the multinational culture of the Soviet Union.

Rise of the reindeer people

(Opposite page, top) *The Yakuts inhabit a harsh mountainous area where reindeer have always provided the necessities of life. Though the Yakuts still live by herding, the opening of Siberia has brought welcome changes:* (opposite page, bottom) *lightweight synthetic-fabric tents, sunglasses and books;* (above) *various livestock services via helicopter, and* (right) *an economy that allows the Yakuts to buy items like western-style clothing and boots.*

Murmansk, freezing in the Arctic tundra, and Jacksonville, languishing in the Florida warmth, share something in common: the Gulf Stream. Rising near the Florida shores, the Gulf Stream flows northeast across the Atlantic, completing its 6,000-mile journey in the Berents Sea, where its warm waters prevent Murmansk harbor from ever freezing over.

The all-season port at Murmansk is always busy. There begins the Great Arctic Sea Route to the East, and there Soviet merchant and fishing fleets are based. Soviet vessels laden with minerals and building materials sail from Murmansk to America's Eastern Seaboard, the Great Lakes and the Gulf ports, while ships sailing under the American flag arrive to unload their cargoes of excavators, pipelayers and cross-country vehicles destined for Siberian oil fields. During the Second World War, Murmansk provided a base not only for Soviet ships but also for British and American convoys. At the local cemetery, one can see the graves of sailors from the Allied powers, among them Americans, killed during the Nazi bombings of Murmansk and its port.

Today Murmansk is the largest and most comfortable of the world's cities that lie within the Arctic Circle. It stretches along Kola Bay, rising in 3 tiers into the surrounding hills. Murmansk's proximity to Moscow and Leningrad (2 hours by air), its comparatively mild climate and the possibility of good earnings make it attractive to many people. But the city does not at all resemble those Arctic towns where one comes for a year or so in the hope of "making a fast buck." Most newcomers settle in Murmansk for good, enjoying the city's pure, transparent air, a skyline free of smokestacks, indoor swimming pools and the only grass-covered soccer field inside the Arctic Circle.

Murmansk port

(Opposite page) *A visitor approaching Murmansk would notice full-size trees, for, though the city lies within the Arctic Circle, its climate is moderated by the Gulf Stream.*
(Above) *The busy port can be used year 'round with the help of icebreakers.*

American sailors who perished here during the Second World War are buried in the Murmansk city cemetery.

81

(Opposite page) *Atomic icebreakers like the* Arktika *make it possible to ship needed goods over northern routes throughout the year.* (Above) *The S.S.* Pioneer *delivers supplies to a geological expedition.* (Right) *Their work accomplished, the crews of the* Arktika *and the* Pioneer *enjoy a soccer match on the shore of the frozen Kara Sea.*

Through frozen seas

central and local governments. All these groups consider the tasks and may suggest adjustments to details. In addition, ministries report plan targets to agricultural and industrial enterprises. Workers in those enterprises also consider the goals, and often ask them to be increased because, from their intimate knowledge of their own work, they can see possibilities for greater output. Thus modified, the draft plan next goes to the Supreme Soviet of the USSR where, after further work by the standing commissions, the final draft of the 5-Year-Plan is ratified and acquires the force of law.

People in the West are often puzzled about centralized planning of the national economy. How, they ask, can everything be prescribed from Moscow? Why isn't scope given to local enterprise and initiative? But no one in the USSR plans or regiments everything to the minutest detail. Centralized planning presupposes a great deal of initiative by local government and by individual enterprises — in fact, by all those who participate in social production — both during the period when the draft is being worked on and after it has become law. Implementation of the 5-Year-Plan does not preclude but encourages initiative. For example, though the plan must be fulfilled, how to do that at the lowest possible cost is the concern of the actual workers involved. In this they are stimulated by economic factors, such as the state's policy of pricing and budgeting. For example, needed goods that cost little to produce may be artificially priced higher than their actual cost warrants to encourage industry to produce greater quantities. Or industry-wide budgets for wages and benefits may be increased to encourage hazardous or difficult industries such as mining or construction. And at the individual level, there is a whole set of material and moral incentives keyed to the needs of each planning period.

Many development programs — those for the Baikal-Amur Railway zone and other portions of Siberia and the Far North, as well as programs for environmental protection and agricultural land reclamation — lie beyond the scope of a 5-year period. The usual 5-year plans are now complemented by a new system of long-term planning: the Comprehensive Program of Scientific and Technological Progress, which covers the 20-year period up to the year 2000, and the Guidelines of Economic and Social Development of the USSR, which covers the decade-long period to 1990. The new system of planning provides better continuity and enhances consistent implementation of social and economic tasks. History has proved the vitality and efficiency of our central planning and management of the national economy. Despite economic disruptions caused by the Civil War and the Great Patriotic War, our economy has been and still is developing without important crises, depressions or inflation.

On the eve of the October Revolution of 1917, the land occupied by the Russian people was distributed unequally and unjustly. A few thousand landowners of noble birth (pomeshchiks)—the largest group among them the Russian tsar and his family—owned a total of 152 million hectares. In comparison, the 130 million peasants who made up the bulk of the population had a total of 215 million hectares—135 million worked by poor farmers and 80 million hectares that belonged to rich peasants or kulaks, who used hired labor.

The nobility, moreover, owned the best lands; kulaks also were able to buy fertile plots; the poor peasants farmed the worst land. Of the poor farmers, a third lacked even their own farm implements or a horse to pull plow and wagon. Many of these peasants were not landowners at all; they rented land from kulaks or nobles or they lived by hiring out their labor.

Although the bulk of Russia's 159 million population in those days lived off the land, they did not live well. Russia at the beginning of this century was said to be the granary of Europe, and indeed prerevolutionary Russia was a major grain exporter with record exports in 1910 of 13.5 million tons from an average annual harvest of 72.5 million tons. Exports did not, however, represent a surplus. Grain merchants and prosperous landowners were interested only in selling grain for profit. During this period of high exports, grain prices on the world market continued to rise sharply, while the domestic market remained far less attractive. According to official data, in a country which was then the world's biggest grain exporter, 30 million peasants—a fifth of the population—did not have enough to eat. Since grain was then the staple food in Russia, merchants and landowners were exporting what had literally been taken from their country's own starving people.

The injustices that institutionalized unequal land distribution and allowed peasants to starve were a major cause of the Revolution. In the first hours of the October uprising, when the Second Congress of Soviets took state power into its own hands, one of its first acts was to adopt a Decree on Land based on a report by Lenin. This law is one of the most important legislative acts in Russian history. The Decree on Land abolished private ownership of the land, and made all land the property of the whole nation. Altogether, 150 million hectares of privately owned land was handed over to the peasants; land was no longer a commodity that could be bought and sold.

The principle that the land belongs to the whole people had still, however, to be put into practice. The Communist Party had always urged peasants to think of establishing big collective or state farms. As early as 1918 some farmers were doing their work together in communes. A few of the most productive landowner's estates were set up as farms belonging to the state. They were called "Soviet farms" or sovkhozes. The peasant majority had the final say about how public land should be cultivated, and in the early period after the October

Kolkhoz and sovkhoz

Revolution most farmers preferred individual forms of land cultivation to collective forms. Landless peasants were settled on land confiscated from landowners. Others received supplementary plots to work along with the farmland they already occupied. By 1927 there were 25 million small individual farms in the USSR.

People tilled these farms with energy and zeal. Although agriculture had been ruined during the First World War and the Civil War following the October Revolution, small-scale farming brought output close to prewar levels within 10 years. Yet it was difficult for individual farmers to buy farm machinery themselves; even if they could afford a tractor or harvester, they could not make full use of it on a small plot of land. Largely without modern equipment or fertilizers and without the benefits of agricultural science, no amount of labor could produce great results. As time showed, small-scale farming gave no prospect of a qualitative leap forward.

The peasants, seeing that productivity was much higher on the few state and collective farms that were in operation, took the path of enlarging farms on a collective basis by pooling individual plots of land, implements, livestock, machinery and so on (except personal possessions and individual allotments) in a single production association. Mass-scale collectivization began on the eve of the 30's. Large collective farms, called kolkhozes, were established in place of 25 million small farms.

Except for the years of the Second World War, when the main grain-producing and other important agricultural areas of the USSR were the scene of heavy fighting and were uncultivated for a long time, growth rates from the time of collectivization to the present have shown a clear and even dramatic rise. As a result of our socialist transformation of agriculture, farm labor productivity has increased almost sixfold, although even today it lags behind that of the United States (it ranges from about one-quarter to one-fifth the US level). Real income of farm families in the USSR has risen more than fifteenfold. Today approximately 126 million hectares (of a total land area of 217 million hectares) is sown to crops. Grain still takes the lead, with wheat grown on 48 million hectares, barley on over 37 million and oats on over 12 million.

The soybean was introduced on a mass scale in the late 1920's. In those days the biology of this moisture-loving plant was not understood well enough for our introducing it into arid areas. Soybean cultivation, moreover, is a difficult matter involving the use of special herbicides, soil cultivators and harvesters, all of which were then in short supply. Today, although this crop is still not nearly as widespread here as it is in the United States, more than 850,000 hectares are planted in soybeans, and plans are under way to raise the harvest to 5 million tons. Soviet plant breeders develop new hybrids every year; American varieties are also grown.

Huge combines work in tandem harvesting wheat in the Lvov region of the Ukraine.

Korean immigrants first started growing rice along the Pacific coast of the Soviet Union at the beginning of this century. From there, during the 1930's, rice growing spread to the North Caucasus and the Ukraine. Only in recent years has there been a sharp rise in the area under cultivation and the real "rice boom" can be said to have begun. Among the major rice-growing regions are the flood plains along the Kuban River in the North Caucasus. There a network of irrigation systems has been built, and thousands of acres of land that had previously been unsuitable for agriculture have been drained and planted. It is planned to harvest 3 million tons of rice in 1980, of which a million tons will come from the Kuban fields.

Little maize (only 2 to 3 million hectares) is grown for grain because the corn does not manage to ripen fully in our climate. Maize is grown mostly for silage; it and other fodder crops account for more than 67 million hectares under cultivation. From 9 to 10 million hectares are planted with potatoes and vegetables. The main industrial crops are cotton, sugar beets, sunflowers and flax—a total of 14 to 15 million hectares.

Collectivization has resulted in several forms of production associations in agriculture. The kolkhoz is a self-administered farming unit managed by the general meeting of its members, who elect their management board and chairman, usually for a period of 3 years. The general meeting also adopts a plan of work, sets up internal rules for the farm, distributes revenues, formulates a policy of capital investment and handles all other management tasks. The produce of the kolkhoz belongs to the farm. The collective farmers themselves decide how to sell the produce and to whom.

The sovkhoz is a central-government enterprise. It is run by a director appointed by the Ministry of Agriculture. All the property of the sovkhoz and all its produce belong to the government. Like their fellow workers at plants, factories and mines, workers at a sovkhoz receive wages from the government.

Along with the 26,000 collective farms and 21,000 sovkhozes there are more than 9,000 "interfarm" enterprises that represent a third aspect of agricultural collectivization. Interfarm enterprises are set up to provide such services as a feed plant or stockbreeding farm, a fattening complex, mechanized dairy or agrochemical center to a group of kolkhozes or sovkhozes. They are structured on a shares basis, and each belongs to its shareholders jointly. The system of interfarm enterprises has encouraged specialization and concentrated services, thereby making the shareholding farms more efficient and more profitable.

Both the sovkhoz and the kolkhoz are integrated into central planning. The sovkhozes work directly from plans adopted by the government. The collective farm's plans are coordinated with the government plan through the signing of contracts and by a system of price and budget adjustments that balance local needs with national ones.

91

Nikolai Dyachkov and his wife, Alevtina, and their 3 children are members of a typical collective farm in the relatively unfertile area of Russia. Nikolai drives and repairs tractors; his wife is a milkmaid. Their house cost the farm 7,000 rubles to build. It has 3 rooms totaling 45 square meters, running cold water and a gas heater that also provides hot water. The Dyachkovs, who chose to buy their house rather than occupy it rent-free, paid 35 percent of the building cost. The house and the lot it occupies are now their property.

Nikolai normally works 8 hours a day for about 200 rubles a month. During spring planting and fall harvest he has to work longer hours. By decision of the collective farm board, the working day is lengthened during these seasons and payment is accordingly increased by 30 percent. Alevtina has 24 cows to milk by machine twice a day, but feeding the cows and cleaning the stables are other workers' duties. Her monthly earnings average 140 rubles.

The incomes in cash and in kind of collective farmers and workers at sovkhozes are more or less the same. The remuneration of labor at both kolkhozes and sovkhozes is based on monthly payments in cash at established rates plus various supplementary payments for efficient and high-quality work, bonuses and increments for grade of skill and length of service. It is the practice at many farms to make supplementary payments in kind—in grain, livestock feed, fruit, vegetables, fertilizer and so on.

Managerial staff (sovkhoz directors, collective farm chairmen, team leaders, managers of livestock farms and so on) receive fixed salaries. They also receive supplementary payments and bonuses but these are not calculated on the same

principle as those of farmers. A tractor driver, for example, receives increments for his grade of skill and sometimes for length of service too, irrespective of the results of his work. As a rule, the qualifications of a manager are not given a cash value. A collective farm chairman who is a practical farmer with only a secondary school education, another who is a young agronomist newly appointed to his job upon graduating from an agricultural institute and a third farm chairman who has the degree of Candidate of Sciences may all be receiving an identical salary.

A tractor driver receives a bonus for his individual good work even if the farm as a whole has not had big revenues that year (the bigger the farm revenues, of course, the bigger the bonuses). But a member of the managerial staff, no matter how hard he works, will receive a bonus only if the farm operation he is in charge of has had a successful year.

The collective farm makes monthly advance payments to each worker in the amount of his or her average monthly wage. At the end of the economic year, when final accounting of produce sales is completed, the farm workers get a bonus—the "thirteenth wage," usually paid in January. The size of the thirteenth wage for each worker is determined by the collective farm board, and then its decisions are ratified by the general meeting of workers, the collective's highest administrative body.

The board and the meeting consider the quality of each member's work—his labor discipline, initiative and output. Though an idle worker may be deprived of the thirteenth wage altogether, most workers receive from a month's to a half year's earnings. Nikolai Dyachkov and his wife work well; their combined bonuses last year came to 1,300 rubles, and their annual income totaled 5,400 rubles.

Working on the farm

(Opposite page) *The Dyachkovs and their daughters take a winter stroll through their village. Collective farmhouses may be purchased by farm families or occupied rent-free.* (Right) *In summer, machine operators such as Nikolai Dyachkov work in the fields, where lunch is served on tables carried to the site (below). In winter they are occupied in their farm's machine shops.*

Where only half a century ago the land was plowed, planted and harvested entirely by hand, machines now ease the farmer's life and increase his productivity. (Opposite page) *Combines harvest grain.* (Above) *Cows are milked by machine.* (Below) *Fields of cotton are sprayed by helicopter.*

Mechanized agriculture

The Soviet Union, huge as it is, has less cultivable land than a glance at the map may suggest. Many millions of hectares are covered by the Siberian taiga, the Arctic tundra, mountain ranges, deserts and marshes. There is less than a hectare of arable land per person, and although this is a fair amount, industrialization and the expansion of rail and road networks will inevitably reduce pasture and cropland further.

An ambitious program to bring previously undeveloped land under crops was taken in the late 1950's and early 1960's. About 42 million hectares of virgin and fallow lands in Kazakhstan and the western part of Siberia were put to the plow. Agricultural production in these regions is now as significant as that of the traditional agricultural areas of the Ukraine and the Kuban steppes. The average yield of wheat accounts for a quarter of the country's total grain output. Desert and semidesert regions account for one-fifth of the territory of the USSR and are inhabited by one-fifth of the Soviet population. The task of cultivating these desert lands is, therefore, of vital importance. At present, the trend is to emphasize development of grazing lands to increase the breeding of stock, especially karakul sheep.

An example of this trend is the reclamation of desert lands in the Suzak district in Uzbekistan, where there is no more than 100 millimeters of precipitation each year. In summer, this desert region is an oven, while in winter the mercury often drops to 35 or 40 degrees below zero centigrade. There, the Kumkent central-government farm or sovkhoz comes into view from beyond the horizon rather like a mirage. Wide streets are lined with tall poplars and ash; there are fragrant flowers, green orchards and

(Below, top) *The virgin steppeland of northern Kazakhstan was reclaimed for cropland in the 1950's.* (Below, bottom) *The Nikcha settlement in Turkmenia obtains its water from the Kara-Kum canal, which has also made productive agriculture possible in desert land.* (Opposite page) *Along the Volga, construction workers build an irrigation system.*

kitchen gardens. Thirty years ago, the land on which this man-made oasis stands was only desert, and a mere score of wells provided the only water to the entire 46,000-square-kilometer Suzak district.

What made this paradise possible? "Subterranean waters, or, to be more exact, artesian wells," says the sovkhoz director, Kuly Anarbayev. "Hydrogeologists discovered large reserves of fresh subterranean water. Today the district has 253 artesian gushers, 1,300 pipe and shaft wells equipped with water-pumping mechanisms, and 5 reservoirs. The reserves are capable of watering an animal

Reclaiming virgin lands

herd of 600,000 head, as well as creating oases like our Kumkent. The farm alone has more than 1,500 hectares of irrigated land under the plow."

Soviet scientists believe that subterranean water, although perhaps not the most economical (irrigation by river and canal is far more extensive), is neverthe-less a very promising means of transforming desert regions.

Even with such heroic efforts, there is nevertheless a limit to cultivable reserves, and one cannot expect ever again so great an addition to arable lands as that which occurred during the years of the virgin-land project. Emphasis is now being laid, therefore, on more efficient cultivation of lands already under crops. Improved drainage and irrigation, mechanization and modern farm management techniques are increasing our agricultural efficiency. The breeding and cultivating of high-yield crops and new strains of farm animals are both very promising.

97

(Left) *Efficient layouts increase productivity in the cattle-raising unit of a state farm in Byelorussia and the hog barns of a collective farm in Russia (opposite page, top).* (Below) *Cows enjoy a more traditional life at their summer watering place near Moscow.* (Opposite page, bottom) *Fresh eggs are ready for distribution at the poultry unit of the Friendship of the Peoples collective farm in the Crimea.*

The principal task facing Soviet agriculture is increasing the production of meat, milk, eggs, wool and hides. Yet for each region, the techniques that will lead to increased production differ. Animal husbandry in the Soviet Union is a vast branch of agriculture with specific, sometimes unique features in a number of regions. The types of animals raised depend on the customary diet of the people inhabiting a region as well as market needs so that, depending on where one is, cattle, goats, sheep, hogs, and even horses and reindeer are the primary food animals.

Breeding improved strains of farm animals for the rigorous conditions of various areas of the USSR is a challenge, and some Soviet breeders' ideas have been most inventive. An unlikely experiment begun 20 years ago—cross-breeding warmth-loving zebus (Indian cows) with central Russian breeds—has now entered the production stage. Today more than 800 hybrid specimens are living on farms near Moscow, and many others have been established in Siberia, the Asian republics and other regions. They have adapted well to arid conditions other breeds of cattle cannot tolerate and have proved resistant to sudden changes in temperature and to disease. In their third generation the hybrid animals are as productive as the best local breeds and excel them in the quality of their meat. Cattle breeders are particularly enthusiastic about the fact that zebu hybrids' milk has a high fat content—about 4.5 percent.

As an exotic concluding feature we might mention the farms for domesticating elk. So far few results have been obtained, but enthusiasts claim that domesticated elk will provide numerous benefits, especially the very large amount of meat per animal raised to maturity.

Animal husbandry

Arctic cucumbers, tropical oranges

Because the Soviet Union includes so many different climates, truck farming varies greatly from one region to another. (Opposite page) Hothouses beyond the Arctic Circle near Murmansk supply fresh cucumbers all year long and green onions (below) are a major hothouse crop in Vilnius, Lithuania. (Right) Mandarin oranges, a subtropical crop, can be grown on Georgia's maritime plain. (Below, right) Field workers proudly display a fine crop of tomatoes grown on a truck farm in the lower Volga region.

101

(Above) *Collective farm markets may be permanent, modern, well-organized structures that function all through the year or (below) more casual displays such as the open-air market set up during the autumn melon harvest in Samarkand.*

A wide variety of foodstuffs is available in Moscow's state-run stores: (above) an array of pickles and preserves at the Deer Shop and (below) produce fresh from the farm at Nature's Gift Shop.

The distribution of agricultural produce from farm to shop counter in the USSR is similar to distribution in any other advanced country, although the great amounts of food that must be moved and the distances to be covered cause considerable difficulties. Collective and central-government farms maintain contact with either a cooperative or government procurement center to which they send their produce. From the center's grain elevator, refrigerator or fruit and vegetable collection point, produce is shipped either to processing plants or to wholesale distribution centers. From the wholesaler, food is delivered to the shops.

Only fresh, perishable foods such as milk, greens and berries go directly from the producer to the consumer through a truck and rail network (which can also be run either cooperatively or by the government), or to collective farm markets located in towns and large villages. About one-fifth of the Soviet Union's fresh produce (but only 2.2 percent of all food) is distributed through such farm markets, including 6,500 located in cities. Although they are traditionally called collective farm markets, this name is somewhat outdated. Not only collective farm members, but any Soviet citizen can bring the produce he or she has grown to the market. They can also sell flowers, mushrooms and berries they have gathered, animals they have hunted and fish they have caught.

The seller incurs little expense. He pays 20 kopecks a day for a place at a counter; the cost of renting aprons, scales or other equipment is equally low. But there are restrictions. Speculation (the resale of goods for profit, or "profiteering") is prohibited in the USSR; and ordinarily, no one is allowed to sell wine because the sale of alcoholic beverages is a government monopoly in the Soviet Union. (There are exceptions. In Georgia, for example, the republic has chosen to honor tradition by allowing individuals to sell small quantities of homemade wine in local farm markets.)

Strict sanitary control is exercised over all operations at the market. Every market has its veterinary laboratory where all meat and poultry is checked before it goes on the counter, and also hygienists who check all other foodstuffs.

Owners of small subsidiary holdings who live too far from a collective farm market are able to sell their surplus produce to the government through the Union of Consumer Societies. These consumer cooperatives have a membership of more than 62 million people. The cooperatives bear all the expenses involved in food storage, transportation and sale. They also supply their members with seed, saplings, piglets, pullets and bees, as well as such other necessities as fertilizer, pesticides and gardening tools at wholesale cost. The produce from consumer cooperatives is sold through their own markets, where prices are slightly higher than in government-run markets.

Food processing is less developed in the USSR than in, say, the USA. On the one hand this leads to some wastage, but on the other the products sold retain their natural taste and texture. In recent years capital investments in food processing, transportation, storage and sales have been rising steadily. However, these branches need modernization. People in Siberia, for example, would appreciate more fresh vegetables in winter; even in Moscow or Leningrad certain agricultural products are in short supply, not because there is insufficient food, but because of transportation, processing and storage shortcomings.

103

From farm to market

(Above) *Factory ships combine fishing with processing, including canning, freezing and smoking.* (Below, left) *Factory workers gut a fresh catch of salmon. The valuable roe is also processed here.*

(Opposite page, top) *Research vessels, capable of monitoring data from orbiting satellites, contribute to modern methods of locating fish shoals in the open seas.*

(Opposite page, bottom) *A trout farm near Sochi in the northern Caucasus exemplifies the growing effort to cultivate various species of food fish.*

Commercial fishing is very well developed in the Soviet Union. The USSR has one of the largest ocean-fishing fleets in the world. Besides traditional fishing vessels, more and more modern trawlers that combine fishing with processing are being added to the fleet. These factory ships are able to handle up to 300 tons of fish each day, producing tinned fish, frozen fillet and a smoked fish delicacy called balyk. Practically all the labor-intensive processes are mechanized, and all "waste" is turned into fish meal for chicken and other animal feed.

Scientists have improved the Soviet fishing industry in several ways. Exploratory voyages have located areas where commercial species of fish new to the Soviet people—macrurus, saber fish, hake and others—are now being caught. In each fishing ground, hauls must conform with permissible catches recommended by scientists. The time of inexhaustible shoals of fish and of rich catches on the high seas has passed. The world catch has remained virtually the same since 1970, and in many regions fish resources are noticeably dwindling. Soviet specialists hold the view that man's requirements for fresh- and salt-water products can nevertheless be met by artificial breeding of fish, mollusks, crustaceans and algae.

At present, there are about 140 fish farms and acclimatization stations in the Soviet Union. Most of these breeding farms stock inland reservoirs with such valuable fish as sturgeon, salmon and whitefish; but over 50 farms breed their product for the open sea. Much attention is being paid to the acclimatization of new species of fish in the Soviet Union. Newly imported species such as trout, eel, American catfish, buffalo fish and paddle fish have increased the number of species cultivated on fish farms. 105

Fishing fleets and fisheries

For love of caviar

(Opposite page) *Along the shores of the Caspian Sea fishermen trawl for sturgeon in much the same way that generations before them have done.* (Right) *A fine catch of sturgeon from the Volga delta will fetch high prices both for its flesh and for its roe.* (Above, top) *Sturgeon roe is processed and packed at a caviar cannery.* (Above, bottom) *In the Soviet Union caviar is spread on buttered white bread or served with small pancakes called blini.*

On the eve of the First World War Russia held only fifth place in the world in the volume of its industrial output. It lagged behind the United States, Germany, Britain and France. Today the USSR is second only to the US (its volume of industrial output is more than 80 percent that of the US). Britain, the Federal Republic of Germany and France together produce less than the Soviet Union. The economic transformation of Russia, as envisaged by Lenin before the 1917 Revolution, was achieved through the gradual abolition of private property by nationalizing capitalist enterprises. Fulfillment of the program was planned to take several years, because although the working class had come to power, it had neither the necessary experience nor the apparatus to manage the economy. At first, only enterprises that already belonged to the state became the people's property. The bulk of the factories, plants and mines were left in the hands of their former owners.

One step toward nationalizing industry was taken right away, however. This was the introduction of workers' control over production and sales at private enterprises. By early 1918 such control had been introduced throughout the country. At that point, only an insignificant number of private enterprises had been nationalized, mainly those which were of special importance, such as food and defense, or those whose owners sabotaged measures of the new government. An attempt was next made to form mixed enterprises in which the state and private ownership would share in management. This measure failed almost completely because of the insurmountable hostility of the owners. So the government, beginning several years after the Revolution, was forced to resort to nationalization on a broad scale. The former owners were left without the compensation that they could have received had they collaborated with the authorities instead of putting up a stiff resistance to them. All industry is now state-owned.

The newly nationalized enterprises were managed according to a principle called "democratic centralism." Uniform centralized government supervision was combined with local initiative; workers were given broad participation in management decisions. In the years since nationalization, the relation between centralized management and the rights granted to lower management and workers has never been static or immutable. The only immutable thing is the principle of democratic centralism; its specific forms have been and still are evolving to meet the needs of society. The present system of management may be likened to a pyramid. Most economic questions are settled directly at enterprises, at the base of the pyramid. The following story will illustrate. A construction enterprise needed to buy gravel. Management wished to buy the gravel from the cheapest source, only 5 miles away. But some distance farther was another gravel pit, and in that community there was also a kindergarten used by children throughout the area. Were the community to receive additional money through the sale of gravel, 109

Roads of industry

it would be able to allot some of it to needed improvements of the kindergarten. The general meeting at the construction enterprise voted to override management preferences, and in this they were supported by a similar vote in the village soviet. Thus at the base level both in industry and within the community, people were able to decide for themselves that the less selfish, though more expensive, purchase of gravel was of greater benefit.

The nearer to the top the administrative body, the fewer orders it issues but the more important the issues it deals with. As for the responsible ministry, or the USSR Council of Ministers and their planning agency, Gosplan, at the very top, they have to determine the main directions and key tasks for the work at hand. Sixty percent of industry profits go directly to the central government for the USSR national budget. The remaining profit is used in various ways. Local soviets may allocate profits from industries in their area, either to force improvements to the plant or factory or to benefit the entire community through, for example, an antipollution project. Some of the money may be used by the industry for its own expansion or improvement plans (even beautification). And the industry may make part of its profits available to its employees indirectly by building new apartments or providing longer vacations or directly in the form of bonuses.

Industries also pay a levy to the central government on the cost of production (usually 15 percent) as an encouragement to cost control. The levy serves also to adjust profits. In the liquor industry, for instance, prices are kept artificially high to discourage consumption of alcohol, yet alcohol costs little to produce. Were it not for a particularly high levy on that industry, its share of profits would be excessive compared to other industries.

Modern Soviet industry is characterized by increasing concentration of production. For example, small enterprises commonly join production associations which increase efficiency by specialization. Several enterprises, each of which produces a variety of small hardware, may apportion the work between them so that one manufactures only nails, another only nuts and bolts, therefore cutting down on the number of tools and dies required. Because of this tendency, the managerial chain of authority today is most frequently from ministry to association and from association to the individual enterprise.

A crucial aspect of the development of Soviet industry has been the "drive to the East." In 1930, the 16th Congress of the Soviet Communist Party pointed out that industrialization west of the Urals could not be based only on the coal and metal mining that had already been developed nearby. To speed up our industrial development, it would be necessary to create a second base in the East, tapping the coal and ores of the Urals region and the Kuznetsk basin. The "drive to the East" envisaged using such local resources to establish industries in the Urals, Siberia and Central Asia. Many industries grew up near the coal and iron deposits in previously underdeveloped areas of Siberia. Textile industries and nonferrous metallurgy, again using local raw materials, were introduced into previously agricultural portions of Central Asia. Soviet accomplishments in creating eastern centers for industry in the decade following the 1930 Congress helped the USSR to achieve victory in the Second World War and also to recover from the devastation left in its wake.

But the war was by no means beneficial to the industrial development of the USSR. This country did not, and could not, experience the industrial boom the United States knew during the Second World War. The Nazi invaders inflicted enormous damage to the Soviet Union. One-third of our national resources were irretrievably lost. The USSR did not manage to regain its 1940 economic level until 1948. So much war damage had to be restored in the west that until the 60's the Soviet government could not invest the great resources needed to continue developing the eastern regions of our country.

The vitality of the Soviet state proved so strong, however, that in the period from 1959 to 1965 it was at last able to allot 40 percent of its total capital investment to eastern industrialization. Projects now being implemented in eastern regions would have seemed completely unfeasible only a few years ago. Among the most spectacular programs are those for the development of oil- and gas-producing areas in the western parts of Siberia, the construction of several dozen industrial enterprises on the Yenisei River and the completion of the Baikal-Amur Mainline.

But we cannot rest content with what we have already achieved. The old division of the USSR into industrial regions and agricultural ones, producing regions and consuming ones, has not been entirely erased. There are difficulties arising from the complex structure of the national economy. Each industry, while it is owned by the state and must fulfill each year's government plan, is also obliged to satisfy local needs and so may find itself hustling to balance the demands of two masters. Labor productivity is another question. In the past 5 years, productivity rose by 25 percent. Nevertheless, numbers of workers are still engaged in manual labor for sorting, packing and loading operations because of inadequate small-scale mechanization.

Our country is still experiencing shortages of some goods. Metal, for example, is in short supply. Large chemical fertilizer plants have been built, but some of them are working below capacity due to inadequate supplies of raw materials and gas. These shortcomings are the result of mistakes in planning; sometimes delays in the introduction of new advanced technological processes slow supplies and create consumer shortages too. There are enough resources to do away with all these shortcomings. The main task is to raise the quality of our management to a still higher level. In the 11th 5-Year-Plan period it is intended to effect major transformations in the structure of the whole economy and to ensure a better relation between the branches of the economy and the needs of each region. 111

(Above) *Geologists wave to the helicopter that will pick them up from an otherwise inaccessible region of eastern Siberia.* (Right) *At an iron ore basin in Yakutia, geologists live in a permanent, if simple, settlement.* (Opposite page) *Their work at such settlements includes identifying and labeling numerous rock specimens in the continuing search for new resources.*

112

For many years now the Soviet Union has been conducting a continuing geological survey to discover the extent and locations of its mineral resources. An army of full-time and seasonal geologists half a million strong is now engaged in prospecting throughout the USSR. Under the auspices of the Ministry of Geology of the USSR, Soviet geologists have in recent years discovered new deposits of natural gas, iron ore, molybdenum, zinc and tungsten. They have found new gas fields in Turkmenia, new coal fields in Siberia. In areas near the Baikal-Amur Mainline (and in addition to copper in Udokan, iron in Chara, and coal in Neyungri) prospectors have located complex ore beds at Kholodinsk, only 70 kilometers from the new rail line.

Geologists with the highest scientific and technical qualifications are trained at mining institutes, polytechnical institutes and at the country's major universities of Moscow, Leningrad, Sverdlovsk, Tomsk and Alma-Ata. The period of study is 5 years. Geological technicians, specialists with medium qualifications, are trained at several specialized secondary schools. This already substantial cadre of experts is joined during the summer months by amateur geologists. During the field season, thousands of students work with the qualified specialists. Students find a summer of prospecting exciting and useful— and work in the field pays well too.

Prospecting in the field still involves the traditional tools of the trade—small picks and sorting boxes, field lenses and notebooks. But 15,000 of the geologists are professional researchers using the tools of pure science. For instance, some forecast mineral deposits with the aid of computers and of survey data obtained from earth-surveying spacecraft or satellites. Using modern techniques, certain geological areas characterized by a high probability of minerals can be spotted from space and later mapped in detail with the aid of computers.

Over a period of several years an extraordinarily deep well is being drilled in the Kola Peninsula. Scientists and drilling crews, using a Soviet-manufactured drilling machine that has already enabled geologists to reach a depth of nearly 10,000 meters, have set themselves the task of reaching the 15,000-meter mark. Rock samples brought to the surface from such a depth are invaluable for the study of the physical and chemical properties of the toughest granite layer on earth.

Geologists are penetrating not only the realm of Pluto but also the kingdom of Neptune. Recently the Pacific Expedition discovered a whole series of solid mineral placers (glacial deposits) off the Pacific coast of the Soviet Far East. The Arctic Ocean has revealed tin ore reserves suitable for commercial development. A natural gas field discovered some years ago 60 kilometers from the shore of the Black Sea will one day pump gas by pipeline to the Crimean Peninsula. Scientists in the Ukraine have developed a battery-powered apparatus that sends brief electric impulses into deep-lying beds of rock. Reflected signals help establish the structure of the seabed and the position and formation of rocks within it. Because the equipment is so compact, it can be mounted on a truck, tractor or ship, so it can be used both out on the open sea and nearly everywhere on land.

113

The search for resources

To many people the most exciting prospecting is the search for precious minerals: gold or diamonds and other precious gems. Soviet geologists have had their share of this excitement. Sometimes they find nuggets of gold weighing as much as 15 kilograms right in the field. They are most interested, however, in tracking down the "cheapest" gold—that found as small particles in glacial deposits called placers in rivers, lakes and off the ocean shore. The Irkutsk Heavy Engineering Works in East Siberia has designed and manufactured one of the world's biggest dredges for recovering gold from offshore placers.

More expensive to utilize are ore deposits within the earth. Such ore deposits have been successfully located by air reconnaissance using a new technology based on changes in gamma radiation. The new technique located gold now being mined in the Kamchatka Peninsula, among the most isolated and certainly one of the colder spots in the Soviet Union.

Precious minerals seem often to turn up in hard-to-get-to places. Not far from Lake Rangul in the Eastern Pamirs, at an altitude of 4,000 feet, Soviet geologists have discovered major deposits of precious stones: bright and crystal-clear red tourmalines and blue and golden topazes. The new deposits are in the vicinity of another very rare mineral deposit of yellow, violet and pink scapolites.

Mirny, a town in Yakutia, is often referred to as the capital of the country's diamond-mining industry. Here the Mir kimberlite pipe (a steeply inclined deposit) is being developed along with a group of other pipes named Aikhal, Ukachnaya and Internatsionalnaya. Mirny's rival—a town called Udachny that is now being built 500 kilometers from

Mirny—is beyond the Arctic Circle, where temperatures drop as low as minus 60 degrees centigrade, where the ground never thaws below the surface and where there are no roads. But diamonds are worth going north for, and the Soviet Union, in spite of its climate, has been increasing its output of cut diamonds by 20 percent each year.

A large chunk of quartz is embedded with streaks of pure gold. The coin is about the size of an American dime.

(Opposite page) Handfuls of diamonds are mined in Yakutia from deep kimberlite pipes such as the Mir and the Internatsionalnaya.

Veins of gold, pipes of diamonds

Diggers in the earth

(Opposite page) *Copper, 99.9 percent pure,
is produced at a mining and metallurgical
combine in Kazakhstan.* (Above)
*Oil shale is mined by the open-cut method
in Estonia, using giant "walking" excavators.*
(Right) *Georgian miners work in a deep coal
mine in the town of Tkvarcheli.*

(Left) *A gas-drilling rig in western Siberia taps the enormous resources of the Tyumen region.* (Opposite page, top) *The complex operations of oil refineries like this one at Novopolotsk in Byelorussia, as well as other branches of the petrochemical industry, require the precision of computer control (opposite page, bottom).*

(Overleaf) *An oil refinery under construction in the Urals*

Fueling for the future

In the Soviet Union there is no "bicycle boom," the price of gasoline is not rising, nor are the rates for electricity, gas or oil. The USSR leads the world in coal and oil production and is second only to the United States in production of natural gas.

Hydropower stations account for about 16 percent of the electricity generated in the USSR. When the building of hydropower stations was in its early stages during the 50's, hydropower engineers had many challenging problems to solve. The Soviet Union pioneered the construction of large dams on soft ground, on permafrost and in earthquake zones. These technologies have made it possible to shift concentration from the west to the Asian part of the country, where 82 percent of our hydropower resources lie. Nevertheless, it is becoming increasingly difficult to supply energy, not because of any fuel shortages, but because of the rapid rise in our energy consumption. From 1950 to 1975, consumption of electricity increased elevenfold. The fuel industry absorbs huge capital investment and is becoming ever more costly. Coal, oil and gas have to be looked for farther north and east in areas with poorly developed road and rail systems, severe climate and limited local labor resources.

These increasingly distant sources for fuel exaggerate an already established disproportion in the Soviet Union: 90 percent of known fuel reserves are concentrated in eastern areas, while 90 percent of fuel consumption is concentrated in the west. Although industry is now being shifted eastward, European USSR will remain the main energy consumer until the next century. Therefore, it is advisable to build nuclear power stations; we believe there is no other way out.

At present, nuclear stations supply 10 percent of the electricity generated in the European part of the Soviet Union, a savings of vast amounts of conventional fuel that could not possibly be brought from eastern regions. The combined capacity of all Soviet nuclear power stations now in operation is 11 million kilowatts. The new Atommash Plant in Volgodonsk, one section of which is already in operation, will be the largest facility in the world for making nuclear reactors. The reactors from this and other plants supply the USSR as well as power stations in the socialist community countries.

Our experience has shown that nuclear power stations are reliable producers of electric power. In recent years, however, scientists have become more reserved in forecasting the future of nuclear energy for a number of objective and subjective reasons. The cost of installing and operating nuclear plants continues to rise, and the failure of the newest fast-neutron reactors to prove economical has been disappointing. Ensuring the safety of workers and the surrounding community is expensive. The cost of foolproof safety devices and of water recycling amounts to nearly a half of a station's initial cost. But the people's health and the protection of the environment are most important. That is why Soviet scientists have done a huge amount of work to ensure the safe operation of nuclear power stations.

Atoms for energy

(Opposite page) *Energy harnessed from the Angara River by the Ust-Ilim hydropower station in eastern Siberia fuels industrial development, but western areas rely also on nuclear energy.* (Above) *The Leningrad nuclear power station, part of the power grid that supplies the city with electricity, is operated through large control panels.* (Right) *Technicians are at work within the interior of the Leningrad nuclear power station.*

Factories and plants are managed by a director appointed by the ministry for that particular industry. The director's managerial duties are shared with his deputies and assistants, chief engineers, chief mechanics and chief designers, and include approving the organizational structure of the enterprise, the distribution of personnel, and the adjustment of salaries among workers within the planned wage budget. The work of management is based on the principle of one-man responsibility. However, every member of the work force, whether engineer; technician or laborer, is encouraged to take part in tackling both day-to-day and fundamental problems. Workers hold regular general meetings at their shop, section and team levels to consider production problems, and trade unions too take an active part in management.

Trade unions are organized on a sectoral basis; that is, workers in different trades employed in the same sector of industry are members of one trade union. The union holds frequent production conferences at which both managers and workers air their opinions and problems. Issues concerning production are uppermost, of course, just as they are at the workers' general meetings. Major issues concerning labor and wages on a national scale are decided jointly by the Central Committee of the Communist Party, the USSR Council of Ministers and the Central Council of Trade Unions. Beyond this function, trade unions have several specific powers that directly affect their members. If a trade union committee of a factory or plant decides that management has dismissed a worker without sufficient reasons, it can demand reinstatement. Such reinstatement is not something exceptional, but occurs frequently in relations between worker, union and plant director. The trade union local can also forbid management to employ a worker on overtime, and it can demand the closing down of a shop—or even an entire plant—if it finds that operations are being carried out in violation of safety rules and management is unable to cope with the situation.

There are two kinds of wages at industrial enterprises. Basic salary, scaled according to the qualifications of the worker and the amount of time worked, does not depend on how much profit an enterprise makes. The second kind does. It consists of additional payments and bonuses that depend on how efficiently and profitably a factory or plant is operating. Salaries may take the form of payment per worker or payment per team. In both cases each individual is paid a basic wage according to his qualifications (including the number of years on the job) and the number of hours he has worked. The team method of remuneration is used where people work as a team and where output rates are set per team, as in the case of coal mining or steel smelting. The difference is that the bonus payment paid to the group of workers as a whole is an incentive to efficient cooperative effort, rather than just individual effort. A third form of salary is being increasingly practiced by labor and management. It is called the team contract method

124

How an industry is run

and includes qualitative as well as quantitative production targets. Both sides are finding this method to be to their advantage.

Workers are paid bonuses for meeting plan targets on time, for raising output beyond the plan target and for increased labor efficiency, savings on materials and fuel or improved quality of a product. Managerial personnel receive bonuses when their enterprise as a whole meets the plan target, achieves higher labor efficiency or turns out a growing ratio of high-quality product. Industrial office workers, engineers and technicians may also get bonuses for devising and introducing innovations. The amounts are determined by management and the local trade union together. As a rule, bonuses are paid out of each factory's or plant's wage fund. Every enterprise also has its own material incentive fund, from which it pays bonuses for carrying out assignments of special importance. However, not all bonuses are in currency. There are also housing and sociocultural development funds, which are used for the general improvement of all workers' lives as well as to provide individual incentives. Thus a conscientious worker or one who makes efficiency suggestions stands a better chance of getting a new apartment before anybody else or he may receive a free pass to a theater for the year.

Often workers show initiative by assuming obligations to meet plan targets ahead of schedule or to exceed plan output. These are called "socialist obligations" and take the form of competition between individual workers, between teams within a single enterprise or between enterprises in the same line of work. Such competition is advantageous both to the state and to the workers: the country receives additional output while the workers receive material rewards in the form of bonuses or moral rewards in the form of various honors.

Moral rewards hold an important place in the lives of Soviet workers. Workers may be awarded pennants and banners, or have their names and photographs put up on the Honor Board or their names entered in the permanent Honor Book of their factory or plant. The best workers are awarded government decorations, such as the Order of the Red Banner of Labor and the Badge of Honor, and medals for Labor Valor or Distinguished Labor. The highest award is the title of Hero of Socialist Labor, and those who win it are interviewed for press and radio, appear on television and become national figures as well known as war heroes.

(Opposite page) Leading workers are presented a certificate of honor at a ceremony in the fields of their collective farm. Medals are awarded to the country's most outstanding workers: (below, left to right) Order of the Badge of Honor, Hero of Socialist Labor, Medal for Distinguished Labor, Order of the Red Banner of Labor.

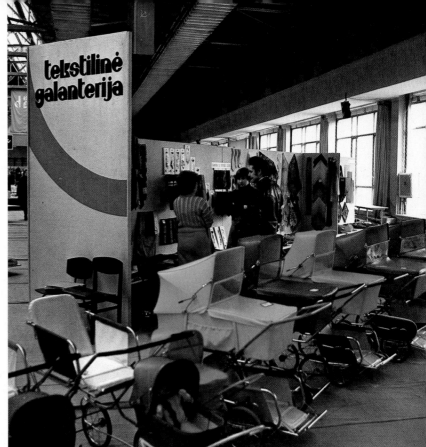

126

(Opposite page, top left) *Color television sets, a popular consumer item, are assembled at a production combine in the Ukraine.* (Opposite page, top right) *Potential customers discuss consumer goods displayed at a local light industry fair in Vilnius.* (Below) *The looms at the Darnitsa textile mill in Kiev are always busy meeting the demand for yard goods.*

In tsarist Russia just before the 1917 October Revolution, merchants' shops overflowed with consumer goods. Because Russia was relatively close to India, China and the Middle East, the range of goods was often wider than in many countries of Western Europe. Yet the majority of the people in Russia, both peasants and townfolk, were extremely poorly dressed—bast (bark) shoes, home-made sheepskin coats, homespun shirts and dresses. There was no question of their buying stylish suits or home appliances; they were simply too poor. Only the ruling classes—nobility, landowners and capitalists—could afford such things.

During the first few years after the Revolution the way people of Soviet Russia dressed did not change. Economic dislocation and famine caused by the Civil War following the Revolution and intervention by the Allied Powers to prevent the assumption of power by the new government did not leave the government with the means to invest in consumer goods industries. First the country needed grain, electricity, locomotives, farm machinery, iron ore and coal. By the time the ravages of that disturbed period had been made good, Soviet Russia sensed the approach of an even more destructive war. Again priority was given to achieving industrial might and a greater military capability at the expense of the people's everyday needs. By the late 30's more attention was being paid to consumer goods; the people were much better dressed and bought various durables comparable to those made in the West.

The war against Nazi Germany halted and even reversed such social progress; once again railroads, electric power stations, factories and plants had to be built to replace those destroyed by war. Only in the 50's was there an upsurge in the manufacture of consumer goods. Despite many shortages of such things as needles, razor blades and fabrics, light industry picked up rapidly, meeting the growing demand ever more fully.

A network of specialty shops is growing and so is buying by mail order and on the installment plan. Lately customers have become more exacting in their demands for quality as well as variety of goods—an attitude explained by a particularly rapid rise in wages and other material benefits such as pensions and bonuses. Several years ago there was a shortage of refrigerators, and people were on waiting lists to get one. Today dozens of models are available, but people are still putting their names on waiting lists because they prefer only the latest roomy and easy-to-maintain models. More than 80 out of every 100 families have a TV set, and they are rapidly replacing their black-and-white sets with high-quality color sets.

Consumer demand for cars has not yet been satisfied, despite the fact that in 1979 people bought more than a million cars—10 times as many as in 1970. Automobile production rises from year to year, and before long the situation will no doubt be the same as it is with refrigerators.

Rapidly changing fashions, both in clothing and in home appliances, compel planning organizations and industries to react more quickly to consumer demand. Flexibility, in turn, requires sizable capital investment. In 1979, the government allocated more than 2 billion rubles for opening new light industries. Light industry is being helped out by other industries too; even in the defense industry, 42 percent of output goes to meet civilian needs such as wire insulation and even casseroles.

127

Good news for consumers

The USSR is one huge construction site. Far from developed areas, where the few roads are bogs in summer and snow in winter, new railroads, new factories, new oil fields and coal mines, and whole new communities are rising where once there was wilderness. Lack of roads and severe climate are the 2 main problems for the technicians, geologists and builders opening up these areas. Air transport, useful to some extent, is too expensive to be the solution. Truck transport is a necessity—with or without roads.

Today throughout the Soviet Union trucks carry the bulk of freight. To suit both the extreme temperatures of the north and its difficult terrain, motor-vehicle industries are turning out a special Arctic version of big trucks. These are fitted with efficient heaters and double windows. The heavy Ural truck produced for these regions has replaced wheels with special track gear than enables it to negotiate boggy terrain. Many Soviet-built tractors have inflated rubber tubes fitted around the caterpillar track for crossing marshland.

At present the bulk of freight arrives at big construction sites in MAZ (Minsk) and KrAZ (Kremenchug) trucks, as well as in the West German multipurpose Magirus Deutz trucks. To provide heavy-duty high-speed trucks strong enough to pull several trailers, the government has built the Kama Truck Works. The KamAZ plant has a production capacity of 150,000 heavy-duty diesel trucks for use on any kind of road surface.

Heavy machinery is also taken to the Siberian taiga forests by rail to help build new railroads. For example, a special diesel-electric railroad crane has been developed to build bridges for the Baikal-Amur Mainline. Its specifications state, "Can operate at 60 degrees below zero."

(Above) *Tractors are assembled on the main conveyor belt at a major factory in Minsk.* (Opposite page, top) *Careful quality control is necessary to achieve perfect precision in a machine shop in Leningrad.* (Opposite page, bottom) *The shovel of a "walking" excavator holds 100 cubic meters of soil.*

Turning out the big machines

The Baikal-Amur Mainline, nicknamed BAM, is the largest construction project currently under way in the USSR. Its 2,146-kilometer track will link the heart of Siberia with the Pacific coast, giving new life to an area that heretofore had no communications with the developed regions of the country. The BAM will traverse a mineral-rich area twice the size of Texas and span 4 time zones.

From the banks of the Lena River and Lake Baikal, the route of the BAM passes over 9 big Siberian rivers, 3,200 streams and 7 mountain ranges, some of which are 2,800 meters above sea level. To erect the 142 bridges and 25 kilometers of tunnels needed will require 80,000 construction workers.

The areas lying in the proximity of the railroad now have a population of about 30,000. In the future, the population will swell to several million. As the railroad tracks are laid, communications systems, including a TV relay network, are laid out too. Recreation centers known as Palaces of Culture, schools, libraries and clinics are appearing in the towns and villages along the railway route. Art galleries are being opened, and local farming is being extended to meet growing needs.

It is planned to set up 9 specialized industrial complexes in the BAM zone, each utilizing local power sources and raw materials for wood processing, metallurgy or coal mining. The railroad builders are confronted with many varied and difficult problems that can be solved only with the participation of numerous organizations. Equipment must be specially designed or adapted to function at very low temperatures. The zone is prone to earthquakes, and the force of a tremor

Building the BAM

(Opposite page) *Far from towns and cities, young workers steadily add new sections of track to the Baikal-Amur Mainline.* (Left) *Electric locomotives are assembled for use in the mountainous portions of the BAM route.* (Above) *Passengers traversing Siberia's vast distances by rail receive courteous attention in well-kept cars.*

is closely related to the condition of the underlying permafrost. If permafrost is destroyed, earthquakes cause far greater devastation. Since builders have to preserve the frozen ground, construction is even more complicated and costly than it might otherwise be. The drop in temperature from 35 degrees centigrade in summer to minus 50 degrees in winter makes special demands on rail quality. Pretempered rails of a very heavy type are used.

On the mountainous western part of the railroad, trains must be hauled by electric locomotives since diesel engines tend to stall at high speeds in the rarefied air. In addition, it is difficult to remove the fumes generated by diesel engines from the extremely long tunnels cut through mountains. To the less mountainous east, 3,100-horsepower diesel locomotives specially designed for the BAM have already been delivered.

Though nature has posed many problems, the human problem is even more formidable. Not only is the manpower requirement enormous, but also people working on the BAM must be given suitable working and living conditions and be helped to adapt to the severe climate. There are 3 main types of workers engaged in the construction of the railroad: builders who transfer from other places, young volunteers sent by the Young Communist League and local labor. An opinion poll has revealed these people's major motives for working on the BAM. In order of priority, they are: the importance of the work for the country, the desire to see new and interesting places, seeing whether one can survive the hardships, personal reasons and (last of all) financial needs.

131

The Soviet shipbuilding industry constructs vessels for many purposes: (opposite page, top) a high-speed hydrofoil passenger ship, (opposite page, bottom) an ocean-going freighter, (below) a floating drilling rig for use in offshore oil operations.

Since the 1940's when the USSR began to create relatively small and structurally simple oil tankers, Soviet engineers have specialized in ships that are unique in world shipbuilding. Soviet high-speed passenger ships, fitted with hydrofoils, have revolutionized passenger water transport. These ships—the Raketa, which travels at 60 kilometers per hour, and the Meteor, which travels at 70 kilometers—are used both on inland waterways and offshore sea routes. Although numerous Soviet rivers, including many in Siberia, are navigable (and fuel consumption per ton of cargo is economical), using the waterways for freight is complicated by two circumstances. First, many rivers are icebound for quite a few months of the year, and second, most of our rivers run north/south, while most freight must travel east/west. Therefore, inland waterway transport accounts for only 4 percent of the Soviet Union's freight, and shipyards produce fewer ships for inland use than for the open seas or other purposes.

In Soviet harbors, floating docks capable of supporting 12,000 tons of cargo and self-propelled floating cranes that can lift loads of up to 300 tons increase port efficiency. Icebreakers have been designed for local use in northern harbors, and in 1959 the world's first atomic-powered icebreaker, Lenin, was launched. More recently 2 even more powerful icebreakers, Arktika and Sibir, have gone into operation, keeping vital northern shipping routes open all winter.

The exploration of outer space has led to the building of special Soviet research vessels for tracking space vehicles, maintaining radio and television contact and receiving scientific data. The latest of this type of ship, Cosmonaut Yuri Gagarin, is the world's largest research ship.

Specialized shipbuilding

A rail trip from Moscow to Vladivostok takes a whole week; no trains at all run to Yakutsk. Few people can afford the luxury of a weeklong train ride, and if you want to get to Yakutsk you have to wait for summer to travel by riverboat, wait for winter to cover the boggy roads with snow—or take a plane. Most people prefer the plane.

Passenger planes flying from Moscow to Yakutsk are always full. They may be carrying a dozen or so families coming home from a holiday in the south; a sales organization employee bringing fruits from Georgia; several scientists putting the finishing touches to the papers they will present at a symposium; geologists with very overweight luggage; a group of cameramen intending to make an exciting documentary about the Arctic; and a concert troupe on a 3-week tour that will take them to forest clearings, new factories and field camps of reindeer herdsmen. Aeroflot, the USSR airline, links almost 3,600 cities, towns and settlements in the USSR. In the past 5 years, the airline carried 555 million passengers.

The IL-62 is regarded as the leading example of the USSR's passenger fleet. It flies to 40 countries and is used for the longer internal routes. A modified version makes a flight from Moscow to Washington in 10 hours with 198 passengers aboard. In 1980 the new wide-fusilage IL-86 aerobus, with a seating capacity of 350, considerably relieved the pressure on overloaded internal routes. A new generation of aircraft now joining our contemporary passenger air fleet includes supersonic liners, compact passenger aircraft and the Supergiant Antheus.

Helicopters carrying as many as 150 passengers fly to areas where there are no airfields for conventional aircraft and are indispensable for carrying freight to inaccessible regions as well. The MI-6, designed by the Mikhail Mil team, can lift 20 tons to a height of 3,000 meters over a distance of 1,500 kilometers, and includes an outboard suspension device that can lift 8 tons. The V-12 can handle a payload of 40 tons, the largest in the world. The multipurpose KA-26 (from the Kamov design team) is, on the other hand, distinguished for its small dimensions. Capable of carrying about a ton of freight over a distance of 600 kilometers, the KA-2 is economical, highly maneuverable, simple to operate and safe (in the event of failure of one of the two piston engines, the helicopter can continue its horizontal flight). The KA-26 can, of course, land practically anywhere.

Wings of the people

(Opposite page) *A large helicopter fitted with an outboard suspension device carries a new house to a settlement along the route of the BAM.*

(Left) *The supersonic TU-144 jetliner will considerably increase the speed of conventional IL-62's on international routes.*

(Below) *Passengers board their flight at an airport in Tashkent, Uzbekistan. Aeroflot links nearly 3,600 Soviet towns.*

(Above) *Nizhnevartovsk is a young town built for oilworkers in the marshlands of western Siberia.*

(Opposite page) *A settlement now under construction along the route of the BAM will soon become one of 20 new towns added to the map of the USSR each year.*

(Right) *Before permanent construction begins, workers are housed in mobile homes. Where there are no roads, the homes are flown in by helicopter.*

mate severe requires great capital investments, an influx of manpower and the solving of technical headaches. Yet definite progress has been made. Formerly, a good part of new development consisted of makeshift dwellings, dreary barracks hastily knocked together. Things have changed since then. Today, right from the start, multistory buildings with comfortable apartments are put up. Development proceeds in an integrated manner: apartment buildings, schools and stores are built simultaneously. Industrial areas are kept well away from residential neighborhoods. In many new Siberian cities, patches of pristine taiga blend well into the city landscape. In one new city in a desert area of Kazakhstan, desalinated water from the Caspian provides both drinking water for its inhabitants and moisture for its greenery. Cities in the Far North are built according to special plans to protect citizens from cold and wind.

The population of such new cities is in some ways unusual. It is extremely varied because the construction work itself draws enthusiasts from all the Union Republics. These enthusiasts are energetic, not rooted to a place, and are unafraid of difficulties. They are also very young. It is not just the romanticism of pioneering construction projects—or the relatively high wages—that attracts these young men and women. As they themselves affirm, it is the significance of the work itself and the benefit it brings.

Jobs are no problem; there is a shortage of manpower everywhere in the Soviet Union. Living accommodation is more of a problem, but taking care of new settlers in developing areas is regarded as a task of national importance. So migration from the center of the Soviet Union toward the new cities to the north and east continues to grow. 137

In the USSR it can be said that new cities spring up like mushrooms. Every year some 20 new cities are put on the map of the Soviet Union, most of them in Siberia, the Far North and Central Asia. Some of them are former villages and small towns that have grown to become cities, but many are built from the ground up and planned from the outset as cities of over 100,000 inhabitants. Building new cities in areas where access is difficult and cli-

New cities from the ground up

The use of prefabricated concrete panels has expedited needed housing construction throughout the country. (Left) *A panel is hoisted into place in Kishinev, Moldavia.* (Below) *Similar prefabricated units are assembled in Neryungri, Yakutia.* (Opposite page) *A new building under construction in Gagri gives workers a fine view over this Black Sea resort.*

Constructions in concrete

(Opposite page) *The brown bear, master of the taiga, still roams the wilderness in large numbers. Other creatures have been less fortunate.* (Above, bottom) *The auroch, once thought to be extinct, is now successfully reproducing under state protection in the Beloveshskaya Pushcha reserve in Byelorussia.* (Above, top) *Young elk are fed formula from bottles by workers on an elk farm in the Kostroma region of Russia.*

The planned character of the Soviet economy plays a big role in the execution of measures designed to protect the environment, restore damaged environments and preserve wildlife. Centralized planning makes it possible to carry out very large-scale measures involving many people, advanced technology and broad organization to protect areas that would remain vulnerable were conservation to be practiced on a piecemeal basis.

An example is Lake Baikal. Among the world's lakes, Baikal is second only to the Sea of Azov in area and, with a maximum depth of 1,620 meters, is the deepest lake of all. Its huge basin holds more than 80 percent of the freshwater reserves in the Soviet Union, and one-fifth the surface freshwater of the entire world. The water itself is pristine, so clear one can see to depths of 40 meters, rich in oxygen even at its depths and nearly free of salts or other minerals.

In modern times ore mining, pulp industries, shipbuilding and fish canning have brought the potential for damage to this unique body of water. Measures to protect Lake Baikal being worked out by scientists of various disciplines already constitute a 7-volume set of scientific recommendations. The entire area is to be preserved as a natural laboratory for studying the evolution and life processes of the approximately 600 plant and more than 1,200 animal species that inhabit the environs of the lake and its waters (and in some cases are not to be found anywhere else). To protect the lake from pollution, scientists suggest that all industrial effluents bypass the lake entirely or, where that is not possible, that industries recycle water. Central planning agencies working with scientists will also be able to control carefully the future growth of industry in the Baikal area. Measures taken so far

have proved successful. An extremely powerful self-cleaning filter for purification plants that service various industries has been tried out at Lake Baikal. It so effectively purifies effluents that they are fit for use as drinking water and the residue of the filtering process is, moreover, suitable for further processing and utilization as fertilizer.

One measure by which preservation efforts are gauged in the Soviet Union is the *Red Book of the USSR*, a major scientific work that lists endangered plant and animal species. Not a single vulnerable representative of Baikal flora or fauna has yet been listed in this work. The *Red Book* lists 63 mammal, 63 bird and 65 plant species that are believed to be threatened with extinction. The color of the page reflects the degree of danger that threatens the animal or plant listed on that page. Red stands for extreme danger: the species is doomed to extinction unless radical measures are taken to save it. White means that the species is not yet threatened with extinction, but its number is so small or its ecological niche so fragile that the situation can suddenly take a turn for the worse. Green warrants optimism. It shows that the tactics man has used to save the species have proved effective. In the past, for example, the auroch (European bison) was not only endangered but actually considered to have become extinct. When a few were discovered still alive measures were taken to protect them, and now the aurochs live in substantial numbers in the Byeloveshskaya Pushcha Nature Reserve in Byelorussia. Musk oxen, also once nearly extinct in this country, have been reintroduced to the Taymyr Peninsula, where a herd is now breeding successfully.

The *Red Book* is more than a mere list of endangered species. It contains infor-

Preservation through planning

mation of great interest to the specialist, including up-to-date data on numbers and distribution of species, reproductive characteristics, causes of population depletion, preservation measures taken in the past and recommendations for measures to be taken in the future. In December 1979 the Council of Ministers of the USSR submitted to the Presidium a preservation and wildlife bill that gave the *Red Book* the status of law. All local authorities will be obliged to protect rare species in territories under their jurisdiction in keeping with *Red Book* instructions. Decisions on new industrial locations will have to be agreed on with scientists specializing in conservation and preservation. Such uniform and widespread control will go a long way toward safeguarding our unique and threatened species.

There are about 120 nature preserves totaling 10 million hectares in the Soviet Union today, and work is under way to open 30 more. In the past, the main function of nature preserves was to protect only certain species, whereas today our aim is to protect the entire wealth of plant and animal life, the whole natural association of life forms. This new approach to preservation is due at least in part to unfortunate experiences. For example, the excessive care lavished on wild deer in the forests of the Voronezh nature preserve included the destruction of wolves, and this resulted in the runaway growth of the deer population. This, in turn, caused the destruction of undergrowth, and its deterioration finally backfired against the animals themselves, many of which died of starvation.

An example of a nature preserve that protects the entire complex of life is the new Taymyr National Park in the extreme northeastern part of Siberia, a stone's throw from the North Pole. The Taymyr Peninsula is a remarkable example of the environment of the Arctic Circle zone. Thousands of polar foxes live in the region, snow rams inhabit the mountains, and it is only on Taymyr that flocks of kazarka, large, beautiful birds of the goose family, can be found.

The USSR includes widely varied geography and climate, and its preserves are equally varied. Two of the newer ones are the first of their kind in the Soviet Union: a marine life sanctuary in the Bay of Peter the Great in the Sea of Japan, and a desert preserve in the southwestern part of the Kara Kum desert. Both these preserves are also research centers. At Repetik, in the desert preserve, researchers of the Institute of Deserts of the Turkmenia Academy of Sciences have worked out a system to halt shifting sand dunes and have thus protected hundreds of miles of highways. The marine life sanctuary, besides protecting the bay's unique ecology, includes a farm for growing sea scallops and oysters.

In 1976, the Soviet government included in its national economic plans a highly expensive item: the recultivation of disturbed lands. Since then, in any project involving disturbance of the soil, the organization responsible for the disturbance has been required to remove the topsoil and store it for subsequent reuse on land that has suffered from open-cut or strip mining. To date the Ministry for the Coal Industry has recultivated more land than had originally been disturbed by coal extraction.

In 1980 a survey of disturbed lands over the entire Soviet Union was completed. The results will help the Ministry of Agriculture to coordinate nationwide efforts aimed at restoring the fertility of the soil.

A young forester works on his day's report deep in the forests of Siberia. A horse is a practical way to get around in the rugged terrain.

Modern conservation measures include the regulation of lumbering to keep timber resources renewed and in top condition. (Below) Sawn timber from selected stands awaits shipment along the Lena River. (Opposite page) Held together in enormous rafts, a timber shipment floats down the Yenisei.

Science and technology in the Soviet Union are guided by the USSR Council of Ministers, and administered by the USSR State Committee for Science and Technology. The committee is headed by Academician Guri Marchuk, a prominent scientist who is also Deputy Chairman of the USSR Council of Ministers. Since all research and design organizations in the USSR (except institutes that form part of cultural organizations) are administered and financed by the state, the USSR State Committee's authority is broad. It includes developing the network of research establishments, financing and supplying them with necessary materials and technical supplies, assigning research and amending current assignments as needed. The committee also supervises the quality of technology nationwide. For example, it is responsible for technical standards in all branches of the national economy, and for proposing how best to utilize new technological developments or theoretical insights.

Coordination of the Soviet Union's international scientific and technical ties and dissemination of data throughout the country's scientific community are also the State Committee's responsibility. Other USSR State Committees have responsibility for such aspects of science and technology as patents and related documents, and state standards for all products from nails and books to airplane engines. Academic standards are maintained through the supervision of the Higher Attestation Commission of the USSR Council of Ministers.

These various government agencies work closely with the USSR Academy of Sciences, the most important institution in the scientific life of the Soviet Union. The Academy of Sciences is an organization of scientists who control their own activities and direct research in many subordinate institutes throughout the country. The academy is composed of four sections: physics and mathematics, chemistry and biology, earth sciences and the social sciences.

Since our socialist society is developing on a planned basis, a major function of the academy is to forecast technical progress as a guide to the future. Forecasting involves both assessing present technology, to predict where it might lead, and selecting objectives, to plan how technology must develop to meet future goals. Integrated forecasting is a rational combination of both forms and is the methodology most frequently used. The USSR has accumulated great experience in scientific and technical forecasting, particularly in the fields of energy, education and fundamental research problems. Comprehensive economic and social development programs have been worked out for a 20-year period for several regions.

Academy of Sciences forecasts are presented to any organization that needs the information in the form of recommendations, frequently offered in several versions. The most suitable version is taken as the basis for guidelines that detail the sequence and schedule by which selected goals are to be met. The guidelines are given the force of law by the Supreme Soviet of the USSR and required funds and technical facilities are provided for their implementation.

Science and technology

Finally, these planning guidelines for the development of science and technology are transformed into specific targets for 5-year plans and for annual state plans. For any suggested project to be approved for an actual plan, its economic validity must be demonstrated. This is, as a rule, much more difficult to do than to prove the purely technological efficiency of a project, because it is not always possible to estimate research costs accurately. The criterion by which the economic utility of research is judged is the lowest possible expenditure and the quickest possible achievement of the desired results. Naturally, in fundamental research no plan can stipulate the achievement of a specific result by a certain date; but these plans can be, and are, specific in concentrating work on certain priorities and in financing that work.

Priority is given both to fundamental research and to research that may lead to practical results in shorter periods of time. Thus in the last 5-Year Plan, plant and animal breeding experiments and research into new biologically active substances for medicine and agriculture were included, as were quantum electronics and the biochemical foundations of life. Short-term practical goals and long-term fundamental ones occasionally merge in breakthrough achievements. Scientists approaching the problem of controlled thermonuclear fusion from very different directions are now coming closer to the long-cherished goal of having an abundance of energy from a virtually inexhaustible source that is harmless to the biosphere. Soviet experts believe the 1980's will be the decisive decade.

The Soviet Union allocates huge sums for scientific research—21 billion rubles in 1980. Besides the USSR Academy of Sciences, 5,000 research institutes, 866 higher-education establishments and thousands of design organizations take part in the work. There are 1,300,000 research workers in the USSR, a figure which amounts to a quarter of the world's scientists and researchers. Our scientific and technical progress makes new demands of higher education. Today no man can master the world's accumulated scientific knowledge. Even if this were possible, that knowledge would not be adequate for long, because new information appears every year. The principal task of our universities, therefore, is to teach future specialists how to enrich their knowledge independently and to develop their ability to find their bearings in the growing flood of scientific information. A student's eagerness to engage in research and to use scientific literature is encouraged from the start.

After graduation from a higher-educational institution, a student may continue to advanced training through postgraduate work either by attending a university or institute or by correspondence with either. The student completes his postgraduate work with the submission of a thesis for a degree of Candidate of Sciences (comparable to a master's degree). The candidate's dissertation is a work of original research, which includes both his own results and a summary of published data in the field. The meeting at which the candidate defends his thesis is attended by official opponents, and anyone present may speak. The final decision is made by secret ballot by the Academic Council at his own school.

A Candidate of Sciences may be a senior researcher in industry, education or other research facility or if he has done well may be given the rank of assistant professor on the staff of an institute or university. Candidates may pursue the even more advanced degree of Doctor of Sciences (comparable to a PhD); the thesis for this degree must be based on fundamental research in the forefront of science. A Doctor of Sciences who is actively engaged in research and teaching may receive the rank of professor. Academic degrees and ranks entitle the person on whom they are conferred to a considerable raise in salary.

Prominent scientists are elected corresponding members or full members of a republic's academy of sciences, a branch academy specializing in medicine, pedagogy or agriculture, or the USSR Academy of Sciences. The academy awards special medals and prizes named after famous scientists for particularly valuable research. The highest awards are the USSR state prize and the Lenin prize.

Physicist Pyotr Kapitsa, a Nobel laureate and member of the USSR Academy of Sciences, is best known for his work with strong magnetic fields.

No single country today can lead in every sphere of science and technology. Wide-scale international exchange of ideas and projects is needed to avoid duplication and save expense. Nor is it possible to solve on a purely national level many worldwide problems of energy, protection of the biosphere and international air, sea and rail transport.

The Soviet Union has always supported any initiative that promotes international contacts between scientists. In 1956 the USSR declassified its work on the peaceful uses of atomic energy at a time when it was ahead of the West in this field (the world's first atomic power station had been commissioned near Moscow 2 years earlier). The active cooperation between the Soviet Union and the United States and Soviet participation in the United Nations program on the peaceful uses of atomic energy by now have a long history of undoubted mutual benefit.

Just as American scientists participated in joint research at the Serpukhov proton accelerator in 1971, so later Soviet scientists joined in experiments at Fermilab, in Batavia, Illinois. In recent years, Soviet and American physicists have jointly studied the structure of elementary particles and have worked on the development of high-energy particle detectors.

The USSR takes an active part in the International Atomic Energy Agency, in UNESCO programs and in international meteorological research. The Soviet Union initiated the European Conference on Environmental Protection, and Soviet scientists participate in most world scientific congresses, conferences and symposiums, many of which are held in our country.

The USSR Academy of Sciences publishes over 300 journals devoted to both the sciences and humanities. In addition, it publishes thousands of monographs (including foreign ones in translation) and collections of articles. Special reference journals contain abstracts on the latest research in other countries in virtually all branches of science. Popular science magazines, such as *Science and Life*, publish their own articles and foreign ones in translation, as well as reviews of current domestic and international work.

Soviet scientists are active in the international scientific community. (Above, top) Drs. Schriber and Mackenzie of Canada chat with Soviet colleagues to their left and right at a forum held in Protvino, Russia. (Above, bottom) US physicists Teng and Courant attended the meetings too. (Opposite page) Basic research is conducted at centers such as the Angara-1 experimental thermonuclear installation at the Kurchatov Institute of Nuclear Power.

(Overleaf) The Tokamak-7 nuclear research facility

International exchange

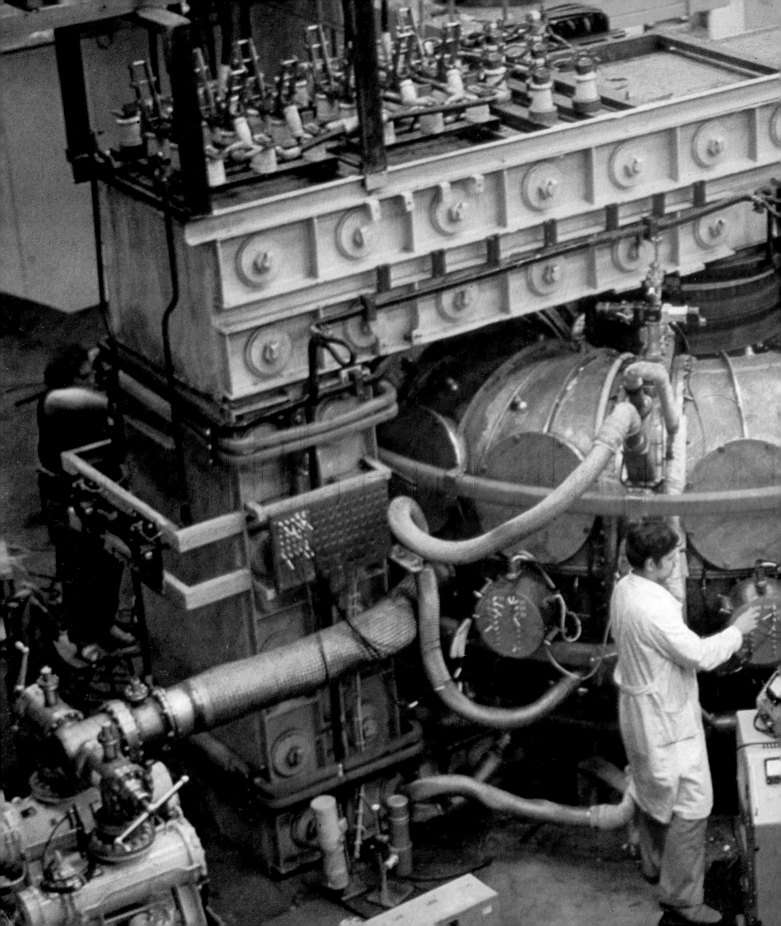

oming up with innovative ideas is one thing; putting them to work to help the national economy may be quite another. One way of accelerating the introduction of innovations in the Soviet Union's planned economy is through scientific-production associations. These associations, under the administrative control of scientists, develop radically new types of equipment and technology and work toward novel products and production methods. Since such associations can tackle all problems from basic research to mass production, they have been introducing new ideas with minimum delay. By 1979 there were 164 scientific-production associations employing 528,000 people. They have had a great influence on our economy through their novel and high quality products.

Science's contribution to the nation can often be measured in numbers: the amount of labor, materials and money saved. For example, extra-hard steel developed for use in low temperatures has resulted in an annual saving of 28 million rubles. Every 10,000 tons of finished product made by new methods of powder metallurgy saves 20,000 tons of rolled stock. The introduction of automatic-couplings in river craft has released 24,000 people from hard manual work.

On the other hand it is difficult to calculate in rubles, man-hours or materials the benefits of introducing highly productive strains of plants and animals. And how can one estimate the effect of developing and introducing the method of subsurface tillage that brought hundreds of thousands of hectares of virgin lands under cultivation without exposing the soil to wind erosion? Practical benefits, measurable or incalculable, in the past and still on the horizon, range from a possible source of fresh food for cosmonauts during long space journeys (the Japanese quail, a small bird that grows quickly and has a high egg yield, is a promising candidate) to advice to farmers about how much fertilizer to use based on data provided by space craft.

The problem solvers

Some basic plant research, while still more exotic than economic, may prove to be of great value in the future. (Opposite page) *Wheat is grown under artificial sunlight at the Leningrad Astrophysical Institute.* (Right) *Controlled environments accelerate plant growth at the Siberian branch of the USSR Academy of Sciences in Krasnoyarsk.* (Below) *Medicinal ginseng root is grown by cell-culture techniques at the Moscow Institute of Plant Physiology.*

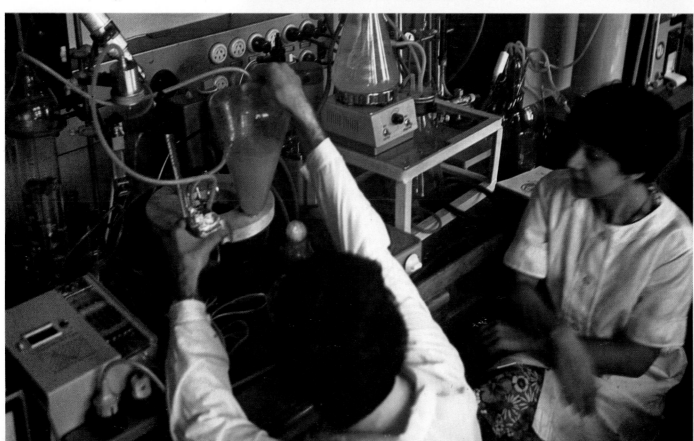

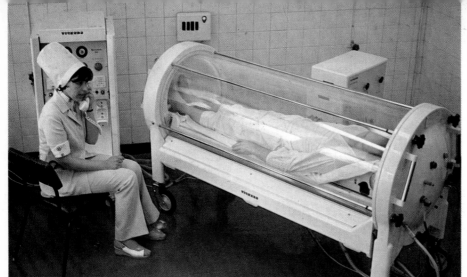

(Left) *A patient is cared for at the cardiological center in Riga, Latvia.*
(Below) *Surgery is performed with the most up-to-date equipment in a hospital in Kiev.*
(Opposite page) *A medical center in Moscow uses hyperbaric chambers to provide oxygen at high pressure to treat such conditions as gangrene.*

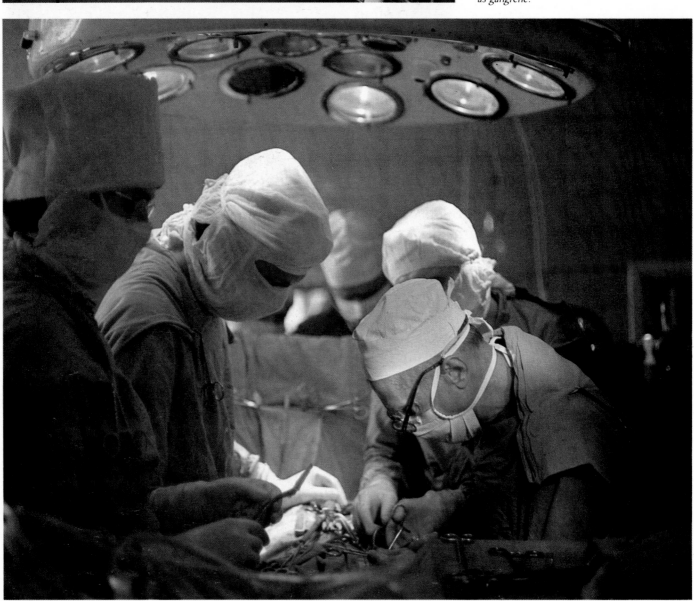

Medical research requires the contribution of many people over extended periods of time. The Soviet Union's present cancer program, for example, is conducted by the USSR and the Union Republic Academies of Medical Sciences and Ministries of Public Health as well as 90 universities and research institutes located throughout the country. Conducting research in this coordinated manner has led to recent technical breakthroughs in Soviet medicine. A new technique in preparing patients for life-saving open-heart surgery is one example. Called hypothermia, the technique involves cooling the patient's body to temperatures as low as 32 degrees centigrade. At such low temperatures, the heart stops beating altogether and blood no longer circulates. Heart-lung equipment, through which blood must be circulated and oxygenated in other methods of open-heart surgery, is not required, but blood is recirculated outside the body as part of the cooling process. Because the body's oxygen requirements are drastically lowered, the patient can survive without damage for a full 22 minutes—long enough for the surgery required in many heart repairs.

Another experimental surgical technique that promises great advantages has been pioneered by Svyatoslav Fyodorov, a Soviet ophthalmologist and director of the Moscow Research Laboratory for Experimental and Clinical Eye Surgery. Surgical techniques developed under his direction have already relieved many people of nearsightedness and obviated their need for eyeglasses. The operation is a very simple one involving reshaping the lens of the eye by making tiny nicks in the cornea surrounding the lens. Using similar microsurgery, Soviet doctors have also had success in correcting the unevenness of lens shape that results in astigmatism. They have found they can not only restore normal eyesight but also improve on nature. Eyesight 150 to 200 percent better than "normal" promises to be of great advantage to people working in such fields as microelectronics.

Advances in medicine

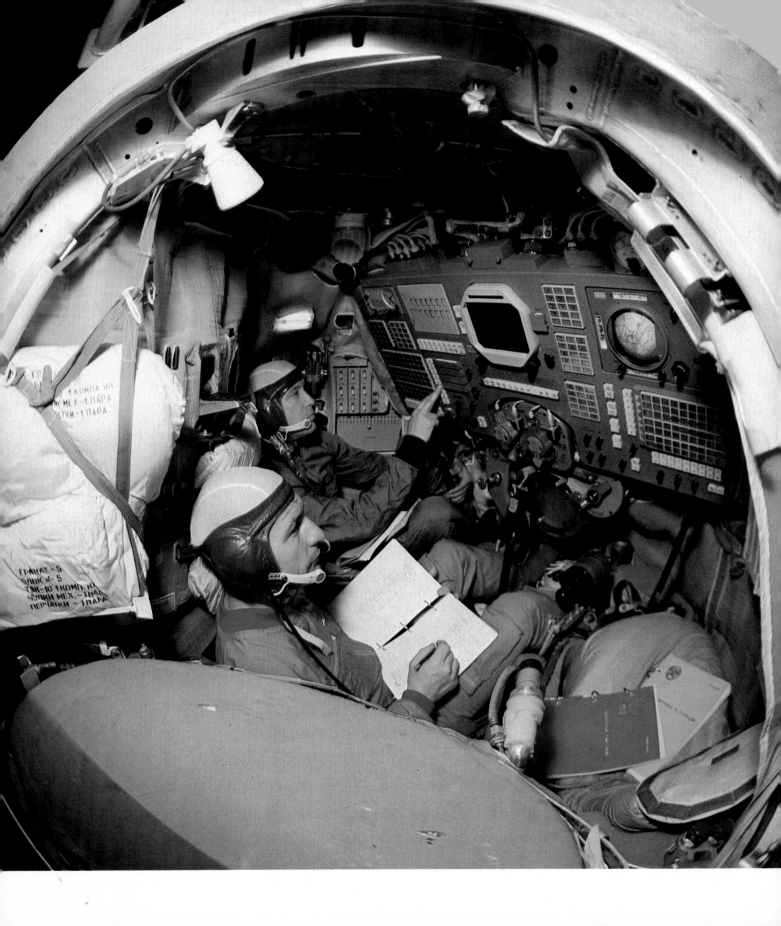

(Opposite page) *Cosmonauts Yuri Malyshev and Vladimir Aksyonov simulate an actual flight during training.*

(Above) *Still in their space suits just after landing from their successful flight, the two cosmonauts relax during an interview.*

When the Soviet Union first sent its cosmonauts on 1-month flights in space, the results were not encouraging. The cosmonauts' bodies did not readapt well to gravity on their return to earth, and the symptoms of dizzyness, weakness and muscle wastage led some specialists to believe that the safe limit for staying in weightlessness had been reached.

Later flights of crews on board Salyut-6 proved this was not so. Specialists in space medicine taught cosmonauts how deliberately to exercise muscles deprived of their usual workload during flight. After many experiments, a special "penguin suit" which increases blood flow during landing was developed. Psychological encouragement from earth also helped the crews of the orbital station. They had regular radio contact with their families and favorite artists as well as the reliable 2-way TV communication with the Mission Control Center. The whole system devised to protect cosmonauts from any harmful effects of weightlessness was devised by a team of scientists headed by Academician Oleg Gazenko. The team was awarded the USSR state prize for its work.

The service life of orbital stations used to depend on their fuel capacity and the power of their booster. The Salyut-6 station considerably extends the life of the orbital laboratory. Its 2 docking modules make it possible to set up a complex that includes the station itself joined by 2 cargo spaceships. Automatic cargo spaceships deliver fuel as needed and everything necessary to ensure normal living conditions for the crew.

Very long flights by crews on board the Salyut-6 orbital station have now become a basic feature of the Soviet space exploration program. Today our experts are confident that space exploration is of considerable benefit to the national economy; in fact results in such technology as space photography of the earth are so promising that the space program will soon be paying for itself.

The Salyut-6 station weighs 19 tons and measures 15 feet long. The whole complex, complete with 2 docked cargo vehicles, weighs 32 tons and is 30 meters long. Two docking units are not by any means the limit, and these weights and sizes therefore give only a starting point for determining the size of future orbital complexes. In many forecasts, their number is growing in almost geometrical progression. Nor does it seem unrealistic to assemble large stations from both all-purpose and specific components while the station is in orbit. The general configuration of the station could easily be changed to suit evolving needs. Looking to the future, we regard today's long flights as preparation for continuous stay in orbit around the earth.

157

Flights into space

(Above) *A model of the Soyuz-Apollo link-up
is a favorite exhibit in the Space Pavilion
of the Exhibition of USSR Economic Achievement
in Moscow.*

158

(Opposite page) *The rocket booster carrying
Soyuz-28 stands ready for lift-off at
Baikonur, March 2, 1978.*

3 LIFE

The 35 years of peace that followed the Great Patriotic War have brought material well-being and comfort to the Soviet people. But a home is not just a roof over one's head and modern conveniences. It is an environment for living; it is an individual world of thoughts and feelings. Today's generation are people with wide horizons and great intellectual demands, people who, now that they enjoy a comfortable life, feel the urgent need to come into closer contact with their traditions and with their cultural treasures. Unprecedented interest in the past is, a logical development of modern Soviet life.

Each of the various Soviet peoples, whether numerous or few, preserves features of its own traditions and customs. Those traditions may be in the form of a craft unique to that people, or the steps of a dance, embroidery motifs, the way a festival is celebrated or a favorite food prepared. Each, while treasuring and safeguarding its own historical roots, greatly respects the cultural heritage of others and feels an obligation to care for its preservation. Thus when the city of Tashkent was destroyed by an earthquake in 1964, people from all over the Soviet Union joined in the effort to rebuild it. Russians, Estonians, Ukrainians and many others each brought their own building materials and rebuilt a particular neighborhood. They did not, however, impose their own styles. Tashkent came to life not as a multi-ethnic mosaic, but as a truly Uzbek city. The ornaments on tall blocks of flats are executed in traditional local style; a supermarket equipped with the latest shop fittings looks from a distance like an Oriental palace.

On the other hand, a visit to the shops of Moscow or Leningrad reveals another aspect of this respect for all our cultures. Traditional Moslem headgear (embroidered hats called tubeteika) are sold alongside Russian fur caps. Clay and wood pipes have joined Russian cigarettes, and Central Asian silk combined with synthetic fibers is a newly popular fabric. So whereas each ethnic group is free to preserve its own traditions within its own land, the traditions themselves are spreading over the entire nation.

This movement toward both preservation and dispersal is encouraged by the USSR government. The USSR Ministry of Culture licenses thousands of craftsmen to make and sell traditional wares and also sets up schools in which these ancient skills are handed down from generation to generation. The Ministry of Culture also allocates money to support folk-dance troupes all over the nation and actively promotes choral singing through all the media. When the government falls short of the general expectations in regard to supporting tradition, there is a great outcry. For example, during occasional shortages of balalaika strings, the newspapers are deluged with complaints. This instru-
162   ment is not only a symbol of the past; it is played by many people even today.

Other symbols have changed their meanings over the years, but are still incorporated into modern life. The troika, a sleigh pulled by three horses, was once a symbol of the wealthy because only they could afford to show off so many horses for one small sleigh. Now troika races have become a traditional sport among the public, and the troika is commonly used as a trademark on products intended for the masses.

Songs, styles, and dances are indestructible, but preserving the material aspects of our culture has been a difficult job. The vital strength and national wealth of any country lie not only in its traditions but also in its historic artifacts. In an attempt to destroy that Soviet strength and wealth, the German Nazi invaders blew up or burned our museums, palaces and churches; they stole cultural treasures and destroyed historical documents and works of art. It was a deliberate plan to destroy this nation's culture, to undermine our people's spirit, pride and national consciousness.

Since the Second World War, preservation and restoration have become a way of life. In the Russian Federation alone, 26,000 historic sites are under state protection. These days, however, the vast extent and high rate of building in the Soviet Union poses a new danger to the historic appearance of old towns. To preserve historic centers, a unique Red Book listing 119 ancient cities and towns has been compiled. Neither new building nor reconstruction can be undertaken in listed sites until all the ancient monuments have received official certificates guaranteeing their inviolability. Where preservation is not sufficient, ancient and historic buildings are restored. Restoration is saving the architectural heritage of every republic in the Soviet Union, and plans for such work have been specified up to the year 1990.

Just as the cultural treasures of the Soviet Union are cared for, so is the cultural life of its peoples. The unique inner town of Ichan-Kala in the city of Khiva, Uzbekistan, looks the same today as it did many centuries ago. But Ichan-Kala is not a dead town with silent palaces, minarets and madrasahs (Muslim schools). Its narrow streets ring with children's voices; there is the buzz of a motley Oriental bazaar. In the shade near the blue-tiled baths, old men in bright robes rest at ease, engaged in leisurely conversation. The voice of the muezzin, calling the faithful to worship, carries far into the distance. Yet those who live in Ichan-Kala, like Soviet citizens everywhere, will also watch the late news on television or attend a meeting at their factory or office, for they are as much a part of the modern world as anyone. Soviet life today has integrated its past into a vigorous and optimistic present.

163

There is no such profession in the USSR as a deputy to a soviet. After election to a soviet at any level, from village to the Supreme Soviet of the USSR, a deputy continues to work at his usual job. Although deputies are given paid leave for time spent attending sessions, they receive no salary in their role as deputy. Such a system makes it possible for a deputy to be always among his constituents, to share their interests and to remain aware of their needs.

In general, the composition of any soviet of deputies reflects the social structure of our society. Workers and farmers, who make up the majority of the country's population, made up 69 percent of the deputies to the local soviets that were elected in February of 1980. Almost half the local deputies are women, and a third are less than 30 years old. The majority, or 57 percent, are not members of the Communist Party. There are, moreover, local deputies from every one of the indigenous peoples inhabiting the Soviet Union.

Deputies are elected on the basis of universal, equal and direct suffrage by secret ballot. The only qualification a nominee must meet is age: to be eligible for election to the Supreme Soviet of the USSR a citizen must have reached the age of 21; to all other soviets, the person must have reached the age of 18.

This does not mean that any person who so wishes can become a nominee. An individual has no right to nominate himself a candidate. The right to nominate deputies is given to trade and professional organizations and collectives of working people—party, trade union, youth, cooperative, cultural and all the other groups that together represent the whole population. As a rule, candidates are nominated at general meetings at which all members of each organization participate and have an opportunity to express their opinions. Even a retired person who is no longer a member of a workers' group may participate in general meetings through membership in a district pensioners' club or local chapter of the Communist Party. The nominating decision is made by a simple majority of votes at a general meeting at the district's leading organization. Naturally, only persons who work well, enjoy the respect of their colleagues and are active in public affairs get nominated.

Elections of the candidates are organized, conducted and controlled—including the counting of votes—by a voting commission of citizens within that election district. All expenses are met by the government, which also provides polling places and information centers, transportation, telephone installations and use of the mass media for speeches before the elections. For the nominees these measures ensure independence (they do not have to rely on funds from any particular groups, or represent vested interests). The voters also have not invested money in any candidate, and therefore, rather than being committed to a single person, they retain the freedom to express their will at the polls.

The relationship between the various soviets reflects the federal structure of the multi-constituent Soviet state. The Supreme Soviet of the USSR and the

May Day celebration on Red Square

165

The Soviet way

Supreme Soviets of the 15 Union Republics and 20 autonomous republics are the highest bodies of government authority. All other soviets, whether they represent few or many people, are called "local." There are more than 50,000 local soviets, all formed in accordance with territorial-administrative divisions of the country ranging from krais (territories that include an autonomous oblast) and oblast (which means merely "area") to district, city, city district, settlement and village.

Local soviets enjoy a broad range of authority. They have jurisdiction within their own area and supervise the work of local industries. They provide free medical service, ensure timely allotment and payment of pensions, maintain law and order, and protect the property, rights and freedoms of citizens. Local soviets also coordinate and supervise the administration of state-owned enterprises. For example, even though a nearby pulp factory may belong to the USSR Ministry of Pulp and Paper, the local soviet can take steps to control pollution or assist in production by such measures as road improvement. Such assistance would ben-efit the local population, which is the ultimate responsibility of all soviets.

Each soviet at a higher level checks whether the conduct of a lower soviet is within the laws of both the republic within which it is included and the USSR, supervises the quality and volume of production and, should disagreements arise between enterprises and local government, is responsible for investigating the problem and arriving at a solution. This combination of general centralized guidance with effective local self-government makes it possible to organize the entire political, economic and cultural life of the country on uniform principles and to coordinate local interests with national ones.

Local interests are most often expressed as mandates—proposals put forward at pre-election meetings and adopted by a majority of votes. Mandates are, in effect, collective instructions from the electors to their deputies. Some are general demands—for instance, to come out for a policy of raising the people's living standards. Others are concrete proposals to improve local conditions.

Zoya Pukhova, deputy to the Supreme Soviet of the USSR, is also the director of a textile factory. Working with the people who elected her keeps her in touch with her constituency. To her right is Nadezhda Golubeva, a weaver and Hero of Socialist Labor.

An example of how the mandate system works in everyday life can be taken from an episode in the Talgar District of the Alma-Ata Oblast in the Union Republic of Kazakhstan. The residents gave their local district soviet a mandate to rebuild their villages and transform them into urban-type settlements. But there were neither sufficient funds at the district level nor the specialists such an ambitious project required. The problem was taken first to the oblast soviet and then to the Supreme Soviet of the Republic. Subsequently, the Kazakhstan gov-ernment assigned an architectural institute the task of working out the recon-struction project. The State Planning Committee allocated the necessary funds and appointed organizations to carry out the plan. In this way the higher bodies of state authority solved a problem which, though mandated by local residents, was beyond the resources of their local soviet.

166 Like this example, most mandates are an expression of policies—the battle

against pollution or the need for better housing—shared by the entire nation. Mandates establish priorities or suggest specific goals; they do not express either the people's or the state's "impossible dreams."

Voters can always check whether their mandates are being fulfilled, because under the Constitution of the USSR deputies and executive bodies set up by soviets are obliged to report regularly on their work to their constituents. Deputies who have not justified the confidence placed in them may be removed from office at any time and replaced by others. Individuals may send letters of complaint to any soviet or speak out in general meetings. These complaints are considered while the soviet is in session, and the deputies, if upon investigation they find the complaints justified, may vote to remove a member. Another election is then held in that district and its deputy is replaced. Within the past decade, electors have recalled more than 4,000 deputies from local soviets.

Mandates are not the only way public opinion is expressed and self-determination is practiced in Soviet life. Standing commissions of soviets study the pros and cons of most major issues before they are discussed in open session, and in this they are assisted by 2,727,000 voluntary helpers. Voluntary organizations include street, house and neighborhood committees; councils attached to cultural, medical and educational organizations, and nationwide groups such as the trade unions, the Young Communist League and other associations. Altogether, the soviets have tens of millions of voluntary helpers from among the people.

Having so many volunteers at times creates confusion or stands in the way of getting things done quickly. Soviet officials must spend considerable time sorting out from the numerous suggestions the most significant contributions, and this problem is constantly discussed in the press. Still, we are proud that so many people are enthusiastic and active participants in decision-making. Volunteerism will perhaps need to be better organized as time goes on, but the help of all our people should surely never be discouraged.

Before taking a decision on any matter, letters on the subject sent by individuals to newspapers and to various organizations and also the opinion of the press must be considered. If necessary, the soviets themselves conduct public opinion polls to guide them in their decisions. When the town soviet of Turtkul, in the Karakalpak Autonomous Republic in Soviet Central Asia, decided to improve the training of young people, the deputies polled the pupils of all 7 secondary schools in the town. The opinions of the majority influenced the soviet to decide to increase admissions to the local agricultural school and vocational school. In addition, the building association responsible for irrigation systems in the Karakalpak Republic was required to set up a training center where young people can now learn to operate bulldozers, excavators and other building machines.

As can be seen from these concrete examples, the soviets have become genuinely popular bodies of state authority.

167

An inclusive image of our nation and its people cannot be accurate without some understanding of the role of the Communist Party of the Soviet Union from the founding of our state in 1917 to the present. Political parties in the Western sense are not comparable. The Communist Party of the Soviet Union (CPSU) embodies to us not only the structures whereby government and international relations are conducted, but also the economic goals, moral standards and social forms to which our people aspire. The party expresses consensus through participation of the masses so that the directions and guidance the party provides for government, art, science and even sports reflect back to the masses an effective version of their own goals.

The ultimate goal of the CPSU is, and always has been, the establishment of a communist society. This task involves molding a new personality in our citizens. Every Soviet citizen in our communist society must be aware of his stake in the common cause, bear a portion of responsibility toward his fellow men and pursue the common good of society through productive work, political participation and personal initiative. To achieve this end the Communist Party in the USSR has worked for many decades to create the material and moral atmosphere in which such qualities of personality can develop to their fullest so that our wish for a communist society can become a reality.

Our course has proceeded, as Lenin envisaged, by historical stages. The immediate goals of the CPSU have changed over the years to correspond to these stages. Each set of goals has been expressed as a program: the First, Second and Third Programs of the Communist Party of the Soviet Union.

The First Program, corresponding to a revolutionary historical stage and embodying the goal of the conquest of political power by the working class, was adopted in 1903 at the founding of the Bolshevik party. This program was realized in 1917 by the success of the October Revolution and the creation of the Soviet Republic.

The Second Program corresponded to a transitional stage between capitalism and socialism. It therefore outlined the basic strategy for constructing a socialist state.

Lenin considered it a central principle of socialist construction that the creative, political and labor activity and initiative of the masses be developed in every way. The old state apparatus was dismantled; in its place a new soviet state apparatus was organized. Members of the party were given key positions in central and local government. Their mission was to implement fundamental democratic changes: returning the land to the people, establishing workers' control over manufacture and distribution, abolishing the previous division of society into estates, assuring political equality and the vote, and promulgating equal rights for women, freedom of conscience, separation of church from state and of education from the church.

The opening session of the Supreme Soviet of the USSR, October 4, 1977.

169

Party of the people

In the economic sphere, the Second Program emphasized raising productivity, developing resources, investing in heavy industry and carrying out electrification. Culturally, party members were obligated to raise the standards of the population in general, and to eradicate illiteracy specifically.

Within 40 years Lenin's vision of industrialization, socialized agriculture and the cultural advancement of the masses as expressed in the Second Program had been achieved. Illiteracy had been completely eliminated. Soviet industrial capacity had grown to first place in Europe and was second only to the United States world-wide. Helped by workers and guided by the Communist Party, our peasantry had accomplished a great economic revolution and created a whole new way of life in the countryside. Moreover, exploitation had been eliminated and new classes of people formed: the Soviet working class, the collective farmers and the new people's intelligentsia which had arisen from among workers and peasants.

At the 21st congress of the Communist Party of the Soviet Union, it was clear that the Soviet Union's progress provided a sure guarantee against the restoration of capitalism within our country. We had entered a new historical stage in which, having achieved the social, political and ideological unity of the Soviet socialist state, we were ready to begin the creation of a truly communist society.

Thus began the struggle of the Soviet people to put the CPSU's Third Program into practice. The Third Program, adopted by the CPSU in 1961 and still our guiding force today, is oriented toward communist construction within the Soviet Union. Thus, for the first time, the party's immediate goals coincide with the long-range task that has remained unaltered for so many years. Three interrelated goals comprise the program: creating the material and technological basis a communist society requires, transforming the social relations of a socialist society into the considerably more demanding ones of a communist society, and molding a new type of person capable of contribution to the advanced society communism envisages.

New directions were clearly called for. The growth of our economy had become so great that methods of planning and material incentives used during the years of socialist construction no longer corresponded to our historical stage, and in fact had begun to retard our development. Therefore, as part of the Third Program during the 60's and 70's, the CPSU raised the scientific level of economic planning, provided greater opportunity for economic initiative and independence of enterprises, strengthened cost accounting, increased incentives, and created more responsive and tighter bonds between technological gains and production methods. This economic reform in general has made production collectives of all sorts more efficient, more responsible for and materially more interested in the results of their work.

The supreme economic aim of the party's Third Program is, however, to raise the people's living standards. Increased prosperity for the masses is one of the means by which the chief social problems in the epoch of communist construction can be solved. We are convinced that through further economic development all classes and groups will be drawn closer together, any substantial distinction between town and country and between physical and intellectual labor will gradually be overcome. Living and working conditions, as well as cultural levels for all people, will be equalized.

With so broad a vision—and so ambitious a program—the guidance of the CPSU pervades all aspects of Soviet life. The party provides the leadership of the governing soviets, economic agencies, trade unions (including creative ones such as the Artists' and Writers' Unions), cultural groups, scientific and technical societies, and sports and defense organizations. CPSU members are expected to exemplify the communist society to which we aspire in social attitudes, moral standards, political participation, patriotism, and industrious work.

These demands are great; yet the standards by which members of the CPSU are judged constitute the strength of the party. The Communist Party of the Soviet Union—its collective mind, unbending will and firm guidance—was the force that laid the basis for the rise of the USSR, directed its development for more than half a century, and now continues to confidently lead it forward. The party is the intelligence, honor and conscience of a new historical community: the Soviet people.

Members of Komsomol, or Young Communist League, arrive at an annual congress.

171

In 1979, in the winter, when the population of the country was least inclined to travel, government census takers visited every Soviet home and every family. All residents of the country were asked to reply, without producing any papers, to 11 questions about such items as age, sex, family status, nationality, and education. One out of every 4 was asked 5 additional questions about number of children, birthplace and migration, place of work, occupation and social category (farmer, worker, or intelligentsia, i.e., professional, managerial or policy-making occupations). From the data gathered emerges a picture of a truly multi-faceted society, unrivaled in ethnic variety.

People of more than 120 ethnic groups were registered. The 1979 census revealed basic differences among the various groupings. Birthrate, for example, varies from 29.2 per thousand among the Tadzhiks in 1978 to 1.2 per thousand among Latvians, though the Central Asian birthrate is gradually falling while the birthrate of the Baltic republics is gradually rising. None of our many peoples, even the smallest and once threatened groups, is in danger of extinction.

The free development of all these peoples was proclaimed in 1917 in the Declaration of Rights of the People of Russia. The Soviet government at that time set about tasks that had not even been considered before: to uproot religious and ethnic animosity and strife, to overcome backwardness, to establish the right to statehood for all peoples and to encourage fully developed economies.

The new Constitution of the USSR, adopted in 1977, may be regarded as a summary of the fulfillment of those tasks. It speaks of the creation of a new historical community which had by then come into being naturally—the single Soviet people, a family of nations. In this family, national features are not ignored nor are they exaggerated. With the continuing rapprochement of their economies, and with the increasing social and cultural interactions among our many peoples, barriers between the constituent populations are becoming obliterated.

Today, integration is a growing tendency. Russian, the common language for communication between all the parts of the USSR, is a factor bringing peoples closer together. As the years go by, the increasing prevalence of marriages between persons of differing backgrounds is helping to abolish any remaining prejudices or aloofness between peoples. In Asia and Kazakhstan the emancipation of women from the strictures of Islam has doubled the trend toward such marriages. Furthermore, although divorce rates in general are on the rise (33 percent at present), mixed marriages are proving more stable than others. This is contrary to the common belief that it is harder to achieve harmony of interests, thoughts and feelings in such families.

Everywhere, as economic development of once-isolated regions continues to attract people from other parts of the USSR, integration in the Soviet Union proceeds steadily without, however, reducing cultures to a common denominator.

173

Cultures and languages

Gradual elimination of all important differences between life in the city and life in the country is a characteristic trend in the USSR. Our rural housing, once devoid of amenities, is now constructed with all modern conveniences. Architects' plans take account of the particular geographical situation and of national traditions, so that some rural housing is 1-family while elsewhere it resembles city buildings of 3 or even 5 stories. Within rural towns one will now find no lack of clubs, museums, schools, libraries and clinics; movie theaters are more and more common. Towns and villages these days are connected by good paved—not dirt—roads, and modern transport and communications connect even remote settlements to the rest of the country.

This sort of progress is necessary to balance the needs of various localities. Where, for example, there is a high degree of urbanization and a danger that the countryside may not receive sufficient manpower, steps are taken to discourage any exodus from the villages by improving the urban quality of life there. Where, on the other hand, there is a labor surplus in the countryside, the teaching of urban trades in the villages stimulates people to move into town, and material and organizational assistance is offered too.

Although the USSR ended private ownership of the land in general and of other means of production long ago, our society still has to cope with the consequences of past chaotic construction that resulted from commercial considerations. Thus it is still true that in the non-chernozem zone of the Russian Federation, the flow of people from rural areas into urban ones is excessive; whereas in Moldavia, the

Although a preference for intricate wood ornaments outside rural homes and gay printed fabrics inside has changed little in this generation, a television set has become a prominent feature in almost every cottage. Houses are still small, however, and a bed in the living room is not unusual. The home to the left is in the Ivanovo region of European Russia; the one to the right in Moldavia.

174

Citifying the country

The Zarya collective farm in the Rovno region of the Ukraine is representative of the move to bring urban amenities to country living. The 5-story apartment houses are indistinguishable from those found within urban centers. Cultural provisions range from large Palaces of Culture to the more modest fisherman's club at a fishing collective in Estonia.

Caucasus and Central Asia, too few people leave the farms in favor of urban life. Planning, although severely interrupted by the war years, is rapidly erasing these unevennesses. Urbanization is proceeding very rapidly.

There are already almost twice as many cities (2,000) as there were in 1939, and from 15 to 20 new ones are added every year. By the year 2000, when the Soviet population will have doubled from 150 million at the beginning of the century to 300 million, another 600 cities will have appeared in now sparsely populated areas. This forecast is supported by precise calculations based on the planned character of our construction and of the whole economy. By then it is thought that fully three-quarters of the population will be urban, compared with the present figure of 62 percent.

At the present time, urbanization of rural areas and the limitation to already urbanized areas is controlled by general plans for each town and city for the next 3 decades and by an overall General Plan of Population Distribution through the next decade. Guidelines exist for even longer periods. Population is expected, for example, to stabilize at between 300 and 400 million by halfway through the 21st century. The growth rate of the Soviet Union will then be zero: the number of births will equal the number of deaths. Problems of urbanization will evidently become simpler; planned solutions will be even more efficient. In the meantime, the basic strategy is to restrain the growth of large cities while controlling the growth of small and medium-size towns so that all our people can enjoy the benefits of urban comfort and culture in town or countryside.

175

The USSR is extremely concerned about the unwarranted growth of super-cities. It is true that of our largest cities none are so immense as New York, London, Tokyo or Calcutta. Yet 9 years ago there were 30 megalopolises; now there are 45. To limit urban growth in these largest cities, new industrial and research enterprises are being located in small and medium-size towns rather than near already heavily industrialized metropolitan areas.

The USSR has some experience in this approach to city planning. Industrial giants built during the last decade—car, truck, petrochemical and nuclear engineering plants—were located near smaller towns which have subsequently developed very rapidly to become large industrial centers. Centralized economic planning, based on the General Resettlement Plan and the General Plan for the Location of Industry, continues to guide the urbanization process by rational disposition of new industrial and scientific research complexes.

The state has also been able to neutralize some of the negative side effects of urban growth. Kishinev, the Moldavian capital, is a good example. As a result of the city's rapid industrial development, it now has more than 130 big factories. Yet Kishinev's pure air and the gardens for which it is famous have not been harmed. All the new enterprises operate on gas, and every plant is fitted with gas and dust traps of new, efficient designs. Parks, gardens and flower beds now cover one-third of the city. Even in such enormous urban centers as Moscow or Kiev, living and environmental conditions are annually approaching the norm recommended by scientists.

Far from idealizing the ecological situation in Moscow, Soviet specialists have drawn up plans for solving the most important problems of environmental protection in the city by the year 1990. Engineers have, for instance, developed a method of recycling water for industry. The first section of an industrial water supply system has already been put into operation; the second section is now being built. In the near future the whole of Moscow's industry and transport will be supplied with recycled water.

Until 1974, Moscow's sewage was discharged into the Moskva River. Over the past 2 years alone, about 100 water purification plants have been built in Moscow, bringing their total number to 1,330. The natural purity of the Moskva River is being restored. The cleaning of the riverbed within city limits is nearing completion, and one can often see anglers fishing there.

Nobody is promising Muscovites ideal quietness, which cannot be achieved in a city of this size. What can be done, however, is to bring noise pollution to the permissible level. City authorities have substantially reduced the amount of traffic in residential areas and near schools and hospitals. Main motorways are lined with trees and hedges wherever possible. The blowing of horns and airplane flights over the city have been banned and construction of the first experimental noiseproof residential building is now under way.

176

(Above) *Kishinev already provides 90 square meters of greenery for each resident, yet the city plans to increase that amount to 120 square meters in the near future. (Opposite page, top) Kishinev's residents enjoy a sophisticated urban life among their many parks and gardens.*

(Opposite page, bottom) *Moscow city dwellers stop for a snack or coffee at an open-air café on Kalinin Prospekt. Such cafés offer a variety of sandwiches and pastries, as well as soda pop, wine and beer.*

Countrifying the city

(Opposite page, top) *The work of city planning takes place at architectural design bureaus such as the one at the Central Scientific Research and Projects Institute of Standard and Experimental Housing Design in Moscow.* (Opposite page, bottom) *A typical result: Troparevo, a Moscow district that has been planned on the site of a former village.*

(Below) *New residential districts in Vilnius, Lithuania, are built at a distance from industrial areas yet are within easy reach of the city center via modern highways.*

Satellite cities, though unusual in other parts of the world, are by now a familiar concept in Soviet city planning. They are built close to large centers—or intentionally at some distance outside—as a base for industries, higher-education establishments or scientific research institutes. The concept helps to control overpopulation in the bigger cities and to reduce concentration of industry close to city centers. Thus Olaine, a satellite city based on chemical engineering, is located 20 kilometers outside Riga. Olaine's products are widely used by factories in Riga.

Satellite cities like Zelenograd near Moscow and Akademgorodok near Novosibirsk are major research centers. The advantage of such research towns is obvious. Researchers are close to their colleagues, and together they can enjoy the surrounding countryside and excellent transport network. Yet they avoid the traffic jams within the city proper. The research centers themselves benefit from nearby sources for industrial and agricultural products.

Surgut and Nadym in West Siberia represent a fundamentally new concept in urban construction. They are known as base cities. Both are located in an oil- and gas-producing region where the climate is most severe. Workers and their families have permanent residences within the base city, but during the working week workers live in "watch settlements" 100 to 200 kilometers from the base city. Scientists have devised a type of housing that functions particularly well in the harsh climate, and the watch settlements are provided with all necessary domestic and cultural facilities. This unique form of satellite city has been so successful that it promises to become a model for urban construction in the Far North.

Planning satellite cities

Although the number of cars in major cities such as Moscow has as much as doubled in the past decade, the population relies primarily on a variety of modern systems of urban transit.

Which form of transport is most popular in Moscow? In terms of numbers of passengers, the answer is the Metro or subway. It carries up to 7 million people daily over its total length of 191 kilometers. After the Metro, the greatest number of passengers—5 million—is carried by buses. In the last few years buses using liquefied gas as fuel have appeared in Moscow. In comparison with their gasoline- or diesel-powered counterparts they are appreciably more economical and cause only a fourth as much pollution. The trolleybus carries 3 million passengers a day along 75 routes, and the "grand old man" of urban transport, the tram or streetcar, another 1.7 million people on local routes from suburban housing to the nearest Metro stations.

The 17,000 (soon to be 25,000) Moscow taxis carry half a million passengers every 24 hours. Other cities are developing unique forms of public transit. Leningrad carries passenger loads of 250 people on its Cyclone hydrofoils between the city center and outlying suburbs. The cities of Kazan and Gorki, both of which stretch for rather long distances along the Volga River, use new high-speed trams.

To make long rides at 75 kilometers per hour quiet and comfortable, the trams feature foam soundproofing and pneumatic shock absorbers that cushion the ride so that it is extremely smooth. Such trams will soon be used elsewhere to connect satellites with center cities.

To meet Siberia's special transit needs, a new bus is now in production. It is painted bright orange for good visibility and is equipped with fog lights. The entire body is a double layer filled with foam for insulation. Should the bus become stuck in mud or snow, the driver does not have to wait for a tow truck to haul him out; the bus's own winch, attached to the front bumper, can do the job.

180

Urban transit

Muscovites have a wide choice of transit systems both within the city and to and from its surrounding suburbs. (Opposite page, left) Trams run along rails while (opposite page, right) trolley buses ride on rubber tires. (This page, right) Most popular is the Moscow Metro, or subway, which features unusually beautiful stations decorated with marble, bronze and murals of mosaic tile. (Below) The Moscow–Kiev highway is part of an expanding road system being built to accommodate increasing numbers of private automobiles and trucking.

The Socialist principle of payment according to quality and quantity of work done allows for differences in salary between one person and another. But social services such as medical care, housing and all types of education are provided free of charge regardless of income level. To help families further, children's clothing and textbooks are sold below cost, and sick leave, maternity leave, retirement and disability pensions are paid out of public funds.

The nationally distributed Soviet state consumption funds which finance health and education are taken out of industrial and consumer sales profits—that is, from enterprises owned by the public. The state social insurance fund, which pays for leaves and pensions, is also part of the central government's budget, but it is controlled and managed by the trade unions. Of this fund 40 percent is provided through allocations from industry and trade and professional organizations. The rest is made up from union membership dues levied at the rate of 1 percent of each union member's wages. Neither industrial, farm nor office workers are required to make direct contributions.

Individual enterprises also have public consumption funds, the amount of which is determined by the collective contribution employees make toward the national income. Therefore, when these funds are distributed—in the form of cash bonuses or housing—the labor contribution of each individual is taken into consideration.

Taxes on citizens play only an auxiliary role in the central-government budget; there are no local or sales taxes. In the 1979 fiscal year personal taxes accounted for 9.2 percent, or about 4 million rubles, of the overall sum. The bulk of the total budget (which was nearly 245 million rubles) was made up of monies received out of profits from state-owned and cooperative sales organizatiions.

The principal tax paid by farmers is the agricultural tax. The amount paid depends on the size of the farmer's plot (not including land occupied by buildings) and the quality of the land (regardless of how the land is used or how much profit the farmer derives from it). The tax rate ranges from as low as 0.3 ruble per 100 square meters to as high as 2.2 rubles per 100 square meters.

Town dwellers earning from 70 to 300 rubles a month pay income tax at rates ranging from a fraction of 1 percent to 13 percent. Those earning more than 300 rubles pay tax at the maximum rate of 13 percent. A tax of 6 percent is charged to childless married women and to childless men (married or not) with incomes of over 70 rubles (sterile individuals are of course exempted). The tax is not paid by women over 45 or by men over 50.

At present, 51 percent of the labor force in the Soviet Union are women, so that in the overwhelming majority of families both the husband and the wife work. The USSR Central Bureau of Statistics regularly surveys the budgets of 62,000 Soviet families. The total income of each family is figured on both payments in money and in kind, and also includes benefits received from public

Moscow's GUM is the biggest department store in the USSR. The initials stand for Gosudarstvennyi Universalnyi Magazin, which means, simply, State Department Store.

Family budgets, town and country

consumption funds. The following chart shows how typical families in town and country budget their incomes.

	Industrial Worker	Collective Farmer
Food	32.0%	34.4%
Clothing and textiles	15.7%	15.6%
Furniture and household goods	6.6%	5.9%
Fuel	0.2%	1.8%
Social and cultural needs	22.8%	14.9%
Rent and municipal services	2.5%	—
Taxes	8.7%	1.3%
Savings and cash on hand	7.2%	13.1%
Miscellaneous	4.5%	13.0%

Outside, GUM's windows are as enticing as its interior displays and, as everywhere, window shopping is enjoyed by passers-by.

183

Soviet fashion designers work with an eye to the future so that the garment industry will have enough time to prepare for new styles and master their production. For example, our clothing experts design fashions that they expect will come into their own in roughly 2 years, and so the fashions that are in the pipeline today are expected to become popular styles in 1983 or 1984.

Once preliminary work is completed, fashion designers hold a conference to work out details for a new catalog of designs and patterns. The catalog is then submitted to the USSR Esthetics Commission for approval. The Esthetics Commission may reject ideas that do not meet their standards, or they may modify styles. The catalog in its final version is printed and distributed to the clothing industry; it can also be bought by interested consumers. The new fashions, which experts have concluded usually last from 5 to 10 years, are then produced on a commercial scale.

Factories operating under the Ministry of Light Industry turn out many styles of clothing and footwear, about half of which are new each year. However, production is still insufficient. At present 184 amalgamated enterprises (a total of 658 garment factories) are in operation, but 13 new ones are under construction and many old factories are now being reconstructed.

The changing tempo and style of life is reflected in fashion, and in the USSR, as everywhere else, young people are quicker to respond to new trends than is the older generation. The jeans boom that arrived from the West some years ago first affected the young and then went on to win over people of all ages. Although no longer the last word in fashion, jeans are so practical and comfortable that they are obviously going to be with us for some time to come.

You can see a wide range of styles in the Soviet Union today: smart suits as well as seedy jeans, hand-painted T-shirts, bright gypsy shawls and traditional Russian sarafans or peasant dresses. Safari-style leisure wear and folk motifs are particularly popular at present, and a return to the fashions of the 40's and 50's is becoming more widespread.

We believe that every item of clothing should be functional and should also be beautifully made. With time, our clothes have become more comfortable and more practical. But in spite of serious preparation, designers are always worried that fashion might develop a whim of some kind and upset the plans of whole organizations concerned with clothes designing. So fashion designers must, like weather forecasters, try to predict the future. So far, however, neither weather nor fashion forecasts can be relied on fully. It is true, though, that today as in the past all nations use similar forms, and these forms alternate from time to time. Analyzing this phenomenon, our designers have come to the conclusion that all the known silhouettes come back at regular intervals. The Ministry of Light Industry of the USSR has suggested that a study of fashion trends as a social phenomenon be undertaken. The problem will be taken up by sociologists, who will attempt to put fashion forecasting on a more solid scientific footing. This would enable industry to tie the caprices of fashion to the needs of the economy.

Fashion forecast

The foods of the Soviet Union are known for their variety and their quantity.
(Opposite page, top left) *Breads and stuffed patties are heaped up for a harvest festival in Moldavia.* (Opposite page, top right) *Children drink kumiss made from fermented mares' milk.* (Opposite page, bottom) *Guests at a Shrovetide festival in Russia bid farewell to winter with hot tea and flat cakes.* (Below) *Shashlik, a favorite snack, is grilled and sold in the streets in Tadzhikistan.*

What are the distinguishing features of classic Russian cuisine and Russian ethnic dishes? First, their abundance. Second, their great variety. Apart from many kinds of meat dishes there are steamed, boiled, fried, baked, jellied, salted, dry-cured and smoked fish (in Siberia people eat frozen raw fish slices), a great number of stews and mushroom dishes, and various kinds of pickled and salted vegetables. On festive occasions dishes are prepared from wild fowl or roast domestic birds. Our soups are famous; for ages Russian meals have begun with cabbage soup (shchi), soup thickened with potato or flour (pokhlebka), fish soup (ukha), soup with kidney and pickled cucumber (rassolnik) or cold soup made from kvass (fermented brown bread) with mixed vegetables and meat (okroshka).

There are so many dishes and beverages in our cuisine that it is impossible to say exactly how many there are altogether. This is easily explained by the vast size of the country, the variety of its climate, flora and fauna, and the influence of neighboring peoples. So the lunch of a person living in the Volga region will differ markedly from that of a Siberian, and even in Siberia itself the frozen dumplings (pelmeni), a Siberian speciality, are in some places made with meat and in others with fish. People in the Far North like reindeer meat, fresh and pickled saltwater fish, rye patties (stuffed with meat, green onions or eggs—or eaten plain) and lots of mushrooms; people in the south fry and bake the wild game of the steppelands, eat lots of fresh fruit and vegetables, bake chicken pies and accompany almost every meal with wine. In northerly parts the cuisine is close to that of Scandinavia and Finland. Among the Don Cossacks there is a marked Turkish influence. Dishes differ, too, even in Central Russian regions lying quite close to one another. Gingerbread—a traditional Russian delicacy—is baked in such totally different ways from region to region that we speak of Tula, Vyazemsk, Voronezh or Moscow gingerbread.

Perhaps the most famous Russian delicacy is pancakes (blini). These are not only cooked in various ways, but also served and eaten differently; some prefer coating them with melted butter, sour cream, jam or honey. Others roll them around a heap of caviar, strips of herring or a morsel of smoked fish.

Non-Russian foods, loved not only by those for whom they are national dishes, but by people from all over the Soviet Union, include Georgian shashlyk, Uzbek pilaff, Ukrainian steamed dumplings with cherries, Jewish stuffed fish, Azerbaidzhan lyulya-kebab (a spicy chopped mutton dish) and Tatar belyashi (beef-stuffed dough fried in fat). The herbs of the Caucasus—kinza, tarkhun and mint—deck festive tables not only locally but in many other parts of the USSR.

In our hurried age, however, cooks (and that means women mostly) appreciate dishes which are quickly prepared. A great help for women who go to work are the specialized Kulinaria food shops which sell many of these popular national dishes in semiprepared form.

For the convenience of tourists visiting what is called the "Golden Circle"—Suzdal, Rostov-the-Great, Yaroslav and other ancient Russian towns—or traveling in the Crimea, the Caucasus, Transcarpathia or the Baltic republics, there are inexpensive but very comfortable roadside cafés and snack bars offering shashlyk (kebobs of a sort), pancakes, fritters, Siberian dumplings or stuffed patties.

Kumiss, shashlik, borscht and blini

The Soviet people have retained the best elements of their old folk celebrations and also created new traditions and festivities. The new national holidays are the Day of the October Revolution, May Day, Soviet Constitution Day, Day of Victory over Nazi Germany and International Women's Day.

The anniversary of the October Revolution on November 7 (October 25 on the old Gregorian calendar) is marked by military parades and general celebrations in the streets and squares. People exchange postcards and telegrams of congratulation, and gather to hold parties in their homes. The press, radio and TV prepare programs about the heroes of the Revolution. Official meetings of industrial workers, farmers and professionals are followed by special concerts at clubs, theaters and concert halls.

As in many other countries, May Day in the USSR is a day of international workingmen's solidarity. It is also a festival of spring. Celebrations are held all over the country; people sing in the streets and squares; in the evening there is general merrymaking and the day ends with fireworks displays.

On Victory Day, May 9, gray-haired war veterans, carrying placards with the numbers of their former divisions and regiments, meet one another in parks and squares. There are many moving scenes as they meet old friends to remember the days of the war and commemorate their fallen comrades. Thousands of people lay flowers on the Tomb of the Unknown Soldier. Radio and TV announce a minute of silence all over the country.

The symbol of International Women's Day, held on March 8, is a mimosa twig. You see it everywhere: in vases on windowsills and in the hands of the people in the street. Men present flowers and gifts to women, to honor them both as sweethearts and as mothers.

Weddings are celebrated with as much generous hospitality as in the old days, although there are some new features too. Though believers may be wed in church, in most cases marriage ceremonies are held at Wedding Palaces in cities, towns and large villages (or at clubs or town hall in smaller villages). The bride and groom sign the register and exchange rings in the presence of their parents, witnesses and guests. The registrar addresses good wishes to the young couple; everyone offers congratulations and toasts with a glass of champagne. Later a large wedding party is held at home or in a restaurant. Quite often the wedding cars go from the Wedding Palace to a war memorial where the couple will lay flowers as a token of respect to the memory of 20 million fallen heroes and as an expression of hope for a peaceful future.

Birthday celebrations vary considerably, but, as a rule, "round-number" birthday parties are large and important occasions and presents are given. Many prefer to celebrate their name day, traditionally the day of the saint whose name one bears. The busiest day in this respect is September 30, the name day of all women called Vera, Nadezhda, Lyubov and Sophia.

One of the good traditions inherited from the past is the celebration of the New Year. Similar to the way Christmas is

Holidays and family celebrations

Along with the new national holidays, Soviet citizens also celebrate in traditional ways. (Opposite page) Outdoor festivals such as the All Trades Festival in Lithuania are very popular, and (right) families still mark personal achievements with delicacies such as caviar and many toasts to suit the occasion.
(Below) Quaint wedding customs are observed to this day in Estonia. The bride and groom must demonstrate to their guests such domestic skills as sawing wood.

celebrated in other lands, every family buys a New Year tree, which the children decorate with toys, mandarin oranges, paper chains and strings of electric lights, and friends and family exchange gifts. There are decorated New Year trees in the central squares of villages and cities.

Different peoples have traditional holidays of their own which they keep in their own way. The Tatars celebrate Sabantui (the festival of the first furrow); the Letts, Ligo (the song festival), and the Moldavians, Zhok (the harvest festival). The Russians mark Shrovetide, originally a Russian Orthodox holiday, as a farewell to winter. It features pancakes, troika sledge rides and merry games.

Christmas, Easter and Whitsunday are Christian celebrations, but you will see many nonbelievers at the churches for the beauty of the rites, and the choirs always attract crowds of passersby. Each religious community observes its own particular rites as it sees fit; according to the separation of church and state decreed in our Constitution, no interference is to be allowed.

The USSR was the first country in the world in which the entire health service was run by the state. Medical care of every sort is free to every person. People receive routine medical care through their area doctor at their local outpatient clinic. The area doctor may be compared to the family doctor because he remains in close touch with his patients for years—or even decades—keeping watch over their health during home visits and at the clinic.

Clinics are equipped to handle preventive medicine, such as inoculation and periodic checkups, and if a person becomes ill, therapeutic medicine. Dental facilities are provided and a dentist practices at every clinic. There is also always at least one mental health therapist to provide outpatient treatment and preventive therapy. Each clinic includes medical specialists on its staff, and as a rule has administrative links with the nearest district hospital. When a patient is hospitalized, his area doctor is kept informed of his progress.

For patients who require more extensive treatment than district hospitals offer, there are large hospitals centrally located in the major cities of oblasts and krais and at the capitals of autonomous and Union Republics. Patients from remote areas are transported to hospitals in major centers free of charge. Mental hospitals for those with serious mental illnesses tend also to be located in major centers, where the expert staff of medical schools and research institutions can participate in patient care.

The Soviet Union also has medical centers that specialize in neurosurgery, cardiovascular surgery and kidney disease. Medical centers are located in the larger cities. If patients cannot be moved so far from their own region, specialists from these hospitals are flown to them by plane or helicopter. Distribution of health services has been worked out on a territorial basis administratively as well as physically. At the district level, the health system is administered by the district department of health under the supervision of an executive committee of the district soviet. At the regional level, direction comes through the regional soviet. All levels within a republic are supervised by the Ministry of Health of that republic. The entire health system is directed by the USSR Ministry of Health headed by the prominent Soviet surgeon and academician Boris Petrovsky.

Patients too ill to work receive benefits during the period of disability. The amount is never less than 60 percent of salary, and increases to 100 percent after 8 years of employment with the same enterprise. More than half the social insurance funds used for benefit payments come from central-government allocations, but the fund is fully controlled by the trade unions even, for example, the amounts of benefits and the length of time they are paid, or whether to pay for some fruit or household help while someone is ill. Maternity benefits include full pay from 2 months before delivery to 2 months after, and the woman's position is left open for a full year after her child is born so she can return to the same job if she wishes. For illness or injury, the duration of the disability period is virtu-

190

Sanatoria are typically spacious, light and airy. (Top) Visitors wait outside the treatment area of the Matsesta sanatorium in Sochi. Receptionists require advanced communications equipment in a large sanatorium like this one. (Bottom) Other modern equipment includes special mobile units such as those used at the Aktyor sanitorium for sunbathing in chilly weather.

The health of a nation

ally unlimited. When a person is sick for a very long time or becomes permanently disabled, panels of medical experts may grant him the status of disabled person. In such cases, the state takes full care of the person through the social security system. If the child of a working mother becomes ill, and the mother must stay home to care for him, her benefits are exactly the same as if she herself were disabled.

There is another aspect to the Soviet health care system that is unfamiliar to many in the West: the sanatorium and health resort network. Large industrial enterprises, for example, run their own overnight sanatoria where chronically ill workers undergo treatment—and receive needed rest—after working hours.

Our trade unions also provide for sanatorium or health resort treatment. If a member of the union or one of his family receives a medical certificate specifying such treatment, his union provides vouchers which usually cover 70 percent of the cost of accommodation, even at the popular southern resorts. However, many people prefer to receive treatment near their homes rather than traveling thousands of miles because the problem of adaptation to the southern climate sometimes reduces the benefit to nil. Therefore there are sanatoria not only in the

Although nearly 90, Professor Yelena Usoltseva is still a practicing surgeon at the City Center of Surgery of the Hand which she helped to found. Those who wish to work beyond retirement age are not discouraged, for an active life is considered healthful.

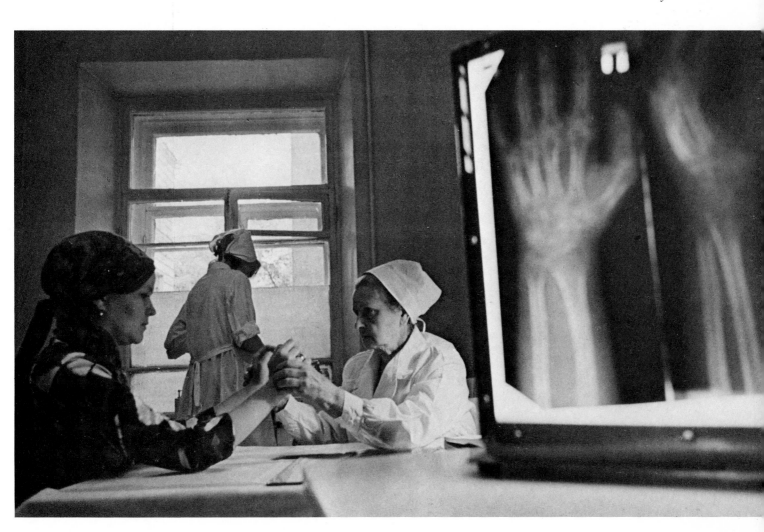

traditional resort areas of the Crimea, the Caucasus and the Ukraine, but also in Siberia, Central Asia and the Far East.

As part of the outpatient treatment of people who have suffered heart attacks, free accommodation at sanatoria has recently been introduced. This is not considered part of a worker's annual vacation, but as temporary disability. In 1979 alone, 30,000 patients received such benefits. Annual vacations are generous in the Soviet Union. The most typical is 1 month of paid vacation; teachers and PhD's receive 48 days, those who perform hazardous work—miners, or workers in the chemical industry, for example—get 5- or 6-week holidays, and for work in the extreme climate of the Far North a 2-month vacation is usual. Only a very few people are given shorter, 2- to 3-week vacations. In addition, vacation homes are maintained all over the country by large enterprises and groups of smaller ones, by trade and professional unions and by the Ministry of Health. These accommodations may be free, charge only a token fee, or 30 to 50 percent of the actual cost (the person must pay his own transportation).

Although holiday homes are scattered everywhere across the land, most can be found along picturesque rivers like the Volga and Dnieper, at the southern seacoasts and the Baltic resorts, and in the beautiful mountains of the Caucasus and Central Asia.

The cost to our enterprises both for maintenance of vacation accommodations and for production time lost during long vacations is high. But the social good of vacations offsets the high cost, and there is no doubt that needed rest and recreation in the long run increase productivity. Average life expectancy throughout the USSR is now 72 years. Only 50 years ago, average life expectancy was almost 30 years shorter. Naturally, a very important role is played by free medical service and extensive health-care facilities, but it is just as important that housing conditions and the standard of living are being continually improved, that educational levels are high and that there is no unemployment in the country.

In the USSR the pensionable age for both men and women is rather low: 60 for men and 55 for women. There are now about 47.6 million pensioners, but of these about one-third continue to work after retirement. Given the manpower shortage, the Soviet Union is interested in making full use of everyone who is capable of working. For this reason, pensioners are encouraged to carry on an active life and are given certain privileges. They can work part time and still receive their full pension, and it is impossible to dismiss anyone simply because of age. This all goes to create a sense of security among the elderly, who feel they can look forward to an active life. Besides, as studies by our doctors and sociologists have shown, work helps elderly people to remain active, and this in turn contributes to health and longevity. There are 20,000 persons older than 100 in the Soviet Union, and about 400 older than 120.

(Opposite page, top) *Going on pension has not forced Anna Maristova to give up her work as a skilled embroiderer.* (Opposite page, bottom) *The effects of an active life can be seen in the trim figures and erect postures of elderly Georgian men who typically reduce their work load only gradually as they grow older.* (Right) *Former steelworker Mikhail Koida chose to retire from his original job, but started a new job working in the hothouses of his steel mill.*
(Above) *All workers have access to holiday hotels such as this one on the Black Sea coast.*

193

For those who like active outdoor vacations, the many climates and terrains of the USSR offer everything from boating (above) to camping (left) to mountain climbing (opposite page).

(Overleaf) *Ski lift in the Pamirs, with Mount Elbrus in the background*

Vacationlands

The USSR has 100 percent literacy. One-third of the population has received at least 10 years of education. This would be impressive in any country, but it is all the more so in the Soviet Union, where only 6 decades ago three-quarters of the population were illiterate, 4 out of 5 children did not attend school, and 50 of our nationalities did not have written languages. As Lenin wrote, "No other country has remained as backward as Russia; nowhere else have the masses of people been so robbed of education, enlightenment and knowledge."

At the beginning of the century specialists estimated it would take at least 250 years to achieve universal education in the country. Those who made the prediction were experts, not amateurs; nevertheless, they were mistaken because they based their estimates on the rate of cultural development in tsarist Russia. Lenin took immediate steps to change that rate. In December 1919, when our Civil War was still raging, Lenin signed a decree on combatting illiteracy. It stated that all citizens between the ages of 8 and 50 had to learn to read and write. Tuition fees in all schools were abolished; millions of children started going to school. Anyone who could read and write was employed in teaching illiterates. A 3-month course in the basics of written language was devised, and facilities for teaching and studying were provided all over the country. Written languages (48 altogether, including Bashkir, Turkmen, Mordovian, Yakut and Nentsy) were created for those who had none. New schools were opened everywhere.

By 1927, more than half the population was literate, and by the beginning of the Second World War illiteracy had been largely wiped out. Within a period of only 20 years, almost 50 million adults had learned to read and write.

According to the Constitution of the USSR, all citizens have an equal right to education. The right is guaranteed by free tuition in all educational institutions and at every level. The right to education is further safeguarded by providing vocational and other specialized schools closely linked with the practical needs of industry, offering evening courses and correspondence schools for working people, teaching a uniform curriculum in the country's many native languages and assuring that all children also learn Russian.

The population actively avails itself of its constitutional right. At present, fully half the population between preschool and pension age are studying, either full time as students or part time to learn new skills while working.

Since nearly half the women in the Soviet Union have jobs, child-care centers are an important aspect of education. There are 122,000 child-care centers at which 14 million children (half of all children of preschool age) are looked after by qualified staff while their parents are at work. Some of these centers are even set up to care for children through the entire workweek; their parents take them home only for weekends.

Children from the age of 3 months to 3 years are looked after at jasli or nurseries. Then they are transferred to kindergarten (detski sad), where they   199

Education for everyone

remain until they start school at the age of 7. The cost of maintaining a child at a jasli is 500 rubles a year, and at a kindergarten 750 rubles a year. Of this cost 80 percent is paid by the state, the remainder by the parents. Families with low incomes or those with many children are exempt from payment. Considerable sums may also be allocated by trade union organizations at collective farms and factories to maintain their own child-care centers.

In accordance with Soviet theories of preschool education, jasli and detski sad are not just places where parents leave their children under supervision. They are educational institutions at which children are introduced to mathematics, foreign languages, music and drawing. Few mothers and fathers could give their children instruction on the scale that is offered by preschools.

The Soviet preschool program by no means results in a leveling of children's development. On the contrary, experienced teachers strive to note the individual talents of each child and to foster those gifts. Children entering school from these kindergartens are as a rule more advanced than children of the same age who have been brought up entirely at home. Nevertheless, while the demand for preschool facilities is still far from fully met and the program is being expanded at an accelerated pace to meet demand, there are still parents who from force of tradition prefer to bring up their children at home.

Along with academic subjects, children are given plenty of time for play and for the development of creative talents. (Above left) Boys enjoy transportation toys in a playground near Moscow and girls and boys (above right) join hands in a ring dance as part of their music lesson.
Even at nurseries and kindergartens children are expected to participate in simple chores. (Opposite page) A child dons white work clothes to help out in the lunchroom of a collective-farm school.

The years of compulsory education have gradually been extended from 4 years in the early 1930's to the present 10-year education. Primary school begins at 7 years of age and continues through the first 3 grades. The remaining years of compulsory education are considered secondary school. After 8 years of general primary and secondary school, children may continue their last 2 years in a combination of general and technical studies.

Parents play an important role in preparing their children for a socially useful life by fostering a sense of civic duty. That role continues after their children enter school. Schools, therefore, maintain close contact with their pupils' families. Parents form committees at every school to take on projects such as visiting families of problem children or improving the school grounds; and there are regular meetings of class parents so that they know their child's teacher, and what is happening in class. Meetings are also held to hear lectures by visiting experts.

Upon completing 10 years of school, students sit for final exams and receive

what is called a school-leaving certificate. Those who fail—and they are very few—get a certificate that states they have attended 10 years of school. The school-leaving certificate gives students the right to apply to any institution of higher education. Admission to higher educational schools is, however, competitive. Those who fail their entrance exams go to work or are called up for military service. After 2 years of either work or military service, young people can again apply for higher education, and sometimes the extra 2 years of experience is a help in passing the entrance exams. Students apply to either a university or an institute. Universities are similar to those in the West, but institutes differ from colleges in that students may continue on into postgraduate work and receive their master's or PhD degree at the same institutes that enroll undergraduates.

The choice of a higher educational school, and consequently a specialty, depends on many factors: family advice and individual inclination, the number of places available and the prestige of the profession. Recent years have witnessed a swing to the humanities. There are several dozen applicants for every 1 place available at art, theater and architectural institutes. Competition for entrance to medical, law and foreign language institutes is also stiff. At the same time, comparatively few people apply to technical institutes to prepare for careers in engineering or metallurgy. This can be explained partly by the fact that girls are reluctant to study those subjects.

The Soviet system of education has been extremely successful. Social progress, however, continually poses new problems, defines new tasks and calls for further improvements. For example, we discuss constantly in the press whether or not to introduce sex education, whether course selection is too narrow and training too specialized, and whether it might not be better for students to have a year or so of work experience before beginning their higher education.

(Opposite page, top) *Mathematics, taught with the aid of simple toys and games, begins even in nursery school.* (Opposite page, bottom, and below) *Discipline and respect for teachers is expressed in the school uniforms worn by both girls and boys throughout primary and secondary school and by the custom of bringing flowers to the teacher on the first day of school.* (Below, right) *This emphasis does not prevent children from having fun during breaks between classes, especially when tempted by the excitement of the first snowfall.*

203

All the general schools in the country, both primary and secondary, have an identical curriculum. We believe that this should be so, for in this way all those who complete the 10 years of compulsory education meet their future at work or in higher education with approximately the same minimum of knowledge. All children with a school-leaving certificate, whether they live in an isolated settlement on the tundra or in a modern apartment in Leningrad, have equal opportunity through equal education.

During the 3 years of primary school, children study the rudiments of their native language and literature, mathematics, history, biology and geography. Primary school children are taught all subjects during this time by a single teacher. From fourth grade on, each subject is taught by a different teacher who specializes in that area.

Although the details of the curricula are constantly modified in response to public discussion and the needs of industry and agriculture, by the time a child completes his secondary education, he or she has had 10 years of mathematics, as well as botany, zoology, chemistry and physics. All children have also studied a foreign language from the third grade on—usually English, but some schools offer French, German or Spanish. Besides the history of the Soviet Union and a course on the USSR Constitution, children will have studied medieval history, the histories of European and other foreign countries, American history and a current-events course called "Political Map of the World." Creative writing is stressed throughout, and worldwide literature (including Jack London and Theodore Dreiser), art, music and drama are studied too. To receive a school-leaving certificate students are tested in all their subjects from creative writing to math, the latter in both an oral and a written examination.

Union and autonomous republics have both Russian-language and local-language schools. Some parents prefer to send their children to a school where teaching is conducted in their native language; of course, Russian is taught as well.

Ten years of learning together

(Opposite page) *Students spend a considerable amount of time in the classroom but, increasingly, labor-oriented activities are being incorporated into curricula.* (This page, top) *Some work, such as placing nesting boxes for birds during the spring, is a popular volunteer activity.* (Bottom) *Students at a Lithuanian school work in the school hothouse, a mini-enterprise that is part of their course work.*

Besides the standard general curriculum which continues through secondary school, almost all Soviet schools these days provide labor-oriented courses as well. Many schools have excellent workshops, and there are also interschool training centers, mini-enterprises that enable senior pupils to choose a trade and begin to practice it under real conditions.

It is not necessary to attend general school for 10 years to receive a complete secondary education. After 8 years, students are given several options: they may stay the additional 2 years and complete their general secondary education; they may enter specialized schools that combine general with technical education; they may enter vocational schools.

Universities form only part of the system of higher education in the Soviet Union. The USSR's 67 universities train specialists in virtually every field in the natural and social sciences and in the humanities; but over 800 other institutes—polytechnical, medical, pedagogical and agricultural—award diplomas in their special fields. Soviet universities have a total attendance of 600,000 students, while the total enrollment at all higher educational schools is over 5 million.

Higher education comprises 5 years of study, and at medical institutes, 6 years. The course of study varies with the student's specialty, but students in every discipline study the history of the Communist Party. The number of humanities courses would be greater for a student majoring in journalism, fewer for one majoring in oceanography. Similarly, entrance requirements vary with the university or institute, and with the specialty chosen.

Once enrolled, students are divided by major interest into groups of 25 to 30 youths who follow the same curriculum in their specialty (hydrology or cartography, for example) as well as the general curriculum of their department (in this case, the Department of Geography, which includes global economics in its scope).

To obtain their diploma, students must pass USSR examinations that qualify a person to practice his specialty anywhere in the country. They must also prepare an original thesis and publicly defend it before official opponents. The student notifies at least 3, and perhaps as many as 5, other universities or institutes of the subject of his thesis, and professionals at these institutes who are experts in that field are free to attend the student's thesis presentation. The student's own university or institute appoints the official opponents, who are also experts in the appropriate field. Anyone present may object to or support the thesis; a central-government commission of educators decides whether or not the student is ready to receive a diploma. Most diplomas have blue covers; diplomas with red covers are awarded to students who have a record of excellent achievement. There is no title awarded with the diploma, but it is roughly equivalent to a bachelor's degree.

Most higher educational establishments—universities and institutes alike—offer postgraduate courses. There are 2 routes toward postgraduate work: excellent work as a student or excellent experience as a specialist in an industry, research institute or technical design office. Postgraduate students of both backgrounds work on promising research problems under the guidance of professors. Postgraduate students who successfully defend their thesis receive the advanced degree of Candidate of Sciences (roughly equivalent to a master's degree

Physics students spend many hours performing experiments in the optics laboratory at Vilnius State University.

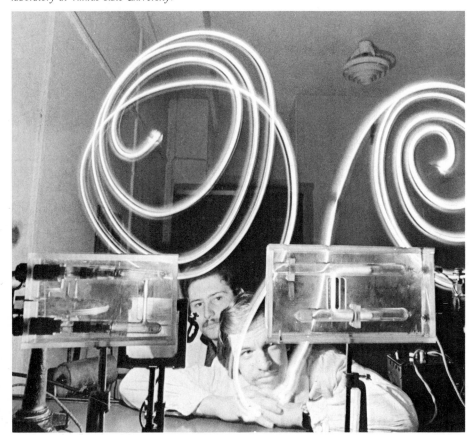

Higher education

in the sciences or humanities). Candidates of Sciences may continue their work toward the highest degree, Doctor of Sciences (again for either the sciences or the humanities).

For students who fail to get into the limited number of places available in institutions of higher education and for those who prefer to start working early to help their families financially, an alternative is tekhnikums, or secondary technical schools, which train people in 490 trades and occupations.

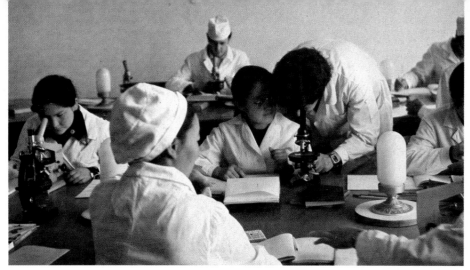

(Above) *White-clad students work in the microbiology laboratory at Kirgiz State Institute of Medicine in Frunze. (Below) Students at the Patrice Lumumba Friendship University come to study from many nations, including those of the Third World.*

Like students everywhere, this young woman at Vilnius University feels free to let go a bit after the last exam.

Technical skills may be learned on the job with the help of veteran workers such as grinder G. M. Ryumkov (left) or at vocational schools. (Below) The village of Leningradskaya has its own agricultural production school where students learn to handle and repair farm equipment. (Opposite page) Gifted children, such as 10-year-old composer Timur Sergeyenya, may attend classes at special schools where their talents are carefully developed. Timur is taught by Vladimir Kuzmenko at the music school attached to the Byelorussian Conservatory.

Specialized schools satisfy the requirement of 10-year secondary education, but also train nurses, preschool teachers and technicians. Vocational schools train children for various trades, but may or may not offer general education. If they do not, students are nevertheless required to complete the 10-year general course by attending evening schools for young workers. As a result of these options, the school dropout is an exceptional case.

Within the secondary school system are other specialized kinds of schools to serve the needs of many categories of students. Most boarding schools are provided to serve children who live in remote areas where population is sparse or people still lead a nomadic life, but there are also boarding schools in such cities as Moscow to accommodate the children of working parents during the week.

A relatively new concept, the extended-day school, has been of great help to working parents. They no longer have to worry about their children while at work, for their sons and daughters have their meals and learn their lessons under a teacher's guidance throughout the working day. There are also specialized schools for the mentally retarded and physically handicapped (the curriculum is easier and longer) and for the gifted. Schools for the gifted allow children of unusual talent to concentrate on such studies as physics, mathematics, music, dance or foreign languages.

Finally, a word about our teachers. There are over 2.5 million of them in the USSR. The figure may seem high—one teacher for every 18 children attending school; the United States ratio is approximately 20 to a teacher—but there is nevertheless a shortage of teachers in some areas of the country. Therefore, the enrollment quota in teachers' training institutes and universities is never reduced, and a graduate who chooses to work in a remote location enjoys quite a few benefits. Teachers, whose profession is probably among the hardest, are traditionally respected by the local population.

Special needs, special schools

Children and teenagers play in the orchestra
of the Palace of Pioneers and Schoolchildren
in Zaporozhye, Ukraine.

A botany group meets to prepare, sort and
classify specimens they have collected
at the Moscow City Pioneers Palace.

At the Moscow Palace of Pioneers and Schoolchildren young girls practice ballet. Ballroom
and folk dance groups are also popular.

Such large children's palaces as the one in
Zaporozhye are likely to include a swimming
pool. The pool is for recreation and for
lessons.

From its earliest days, the Soviet government undertook to care for the all-round development of its citizens, not only their academic training but their creative talents as well. That is why recreation centers that provide for creative interests have become a way of life in the Soviet Union.

For adults there are 136,000 recreation centers (or clubs) throughout the country. For children, there are 4,500 clubs and another 7,000 children's groups within adult clubs. The biggest recreation clubs for adults are called Palaces of Culture, and those for children, Young Pioneer Palaces. Whatever their size, recreation clubs are truly a mass institution where everyone can satisfy the need for creative expression and intellectual pursuit.

Most clubs and palaces belong to the Ministry of Culture and are maintained at central-government expense. More than 20,000 clubs, however, belong to the trade unions and are established at plants and factories for their own workers and students. Clubs at collective farms are established by decision of the general meeting and are subsidized by the farms themselves. There are also clubs for patients at sanatoria, clubs for servicemen, scientists, writers, teachers, architects, actors, composers and film makers.

Perhaps the finest of the Soviet Union's 4,500 youth recreation centers is the Moscow Young Pioneers Palace. This beautiful building in the Lenin Hills of Moscow has more than 500 specialized laboratories and studios, a large concert hall, a winter garden and a swimming pool. The laboratory of experimental biology, with its groups on genetics, microbiology and biochemistry of proteins, enjoys great popularity. The Department of Esthetic Education includes 2 theaters, a literary studio, a studio of painting and sculpture, and a ballroom dance studio. The children's film studio group produces feature, documentary and popular science films and, naturally, animated cartoons.

Adult clubs have similarly ambitious programs and maintain a full-time professional staff. Many of the amateur groups formed as recreation clubs have become quite famous, especially in the fields of music, drama and dance.

Although the arts receive the most attention, adult centers offer many other educational, recreational and social resources. Large Palaces of Culture have swimming pools as well as dance and exercise classes, courses in crafts and hobbies as well as painting and sculpture, chess groups and literary discussion groups and even "Over-30 Clubs" where a first attempt is being made to help single people find partners.

Children display ship models they have made at the Moscow City Young Pioneers Palace.

At the airfield of the flying club of the Nakotne collective farm in Latvia, adults build, maintain and fly their own gliders.

At a Palace of Culture

The Ministry of Culture of the USSR is housed in Moscow in an old building on Kuibyshev Street, a few blocks from the Kremlin. The major concern of those who work there is planning. Planning would seem to have little to do with the arts. Creative work, after all, cannot be planned, for how could you control an artist's interest in a certain topic, his choice of genre or, ultimately, his artistic imagination? Planning is, however, essential to the system of culture as a whole in the Soviet Union. The network of theaters, concert halls, museums and galleries must be planned, and this is true also of the number and distribution of state dance troupes, repertory theaters and art exhibits. At present, it is planned to provide, for example, permanent clubs for every settlement of over 300 people, and this program alone will require an additional 330,000 professionals in various fields. New art and music institutes must be built and existing ones expanded. The dozens of new towns growing up in Siberia need itinerant and permanent art exhibits as well as the buildings in which to house them.

In accordance with the Ministry of Culture's planning goals, the Council of Ministers of the USSR allocates funds to ensure public access to the arts. Consequently, there are no major towns today without a theater or concert hall. New halls—complete with repertory theater groups, ballet companies and symphony orchestras to perform in them—are opening every year from Estonia to the Far East to place culture within the reach of everyone.

Each Soviet republic has its own distinctive forms of music, art, drama and opera, as well as its own contemporary literature and cinematography. In the first years of Soviet government, Moscow and Leningrad sent workers in the arts to the various republics to encourage national elements in local culture. The Khakass, like many other small peoples (there were only 55,000 of them), did not have a written language. When cultural workers arrived there from Moscow in 1925, only 3 people could be found who could read at all. With assistance from Moscow, a written language was devised. Russian choreographers, in turn, learned the Khakass language in order to study local folklore. Using Khakass folklore themes, these choreographers helped to create a national dance company.

These were only first steps. Today, over 100 Khakass writers and critics publish several newspapers and a regularly published anthology of stories and poetry in the Khakass tongue. Their prose and poetry is translated into many languages of the peoples of the USSR, and works by Khakass playwrights are included in the local drama theater repertoire. Khakass graphic artists, painters and metal craftsmen are exhibited in their own museums, in Moscow and in other European capitals. And Zharki, the Khakass national ensemble (both directors, naturally, are Khakass), has been on tours abroad. It is clear to our cultural planners that today there is no longer any need to send experts from Moscow to help our country's "backward" areas.

The policy makers at Kuibyshev Street consider that the 2 jobs of making culture accessible to people and encouraging the development of national cultures

Interior of the Bolshoi Theater

213

Culture popular and classic

are still not enough. The Ministry of Culture also believes it is important to encourage people to take an active part in the arts themselves. There has already been substantial progress: in their free time, over 18 million people take part in some form of amateur art activity. They are members of 160,000 choirs, 140,000 music ensembles, 110,000 drama groups and 20,000 film and photography clubs. The Ministry of Culture, while it does not pay for all the costumes, instruments and equipment needed, is nevertheless responsible for overall organization of all amateur participation in the arts.

A trade union in a particular enterprise is generally very willing to provide funds for amateur art groups. Experience has shown that such activities increase enthusiasm for work, improve the collective spirit and help young people adjust more quickly to factory life. Collective farms have had similar experiences. The Iskra song and dance ensemble is an amateur group from a collective farm on the Upper Volga. Half the collective farm's work force is under 30. Realizing that if some kind of interesting activity were not organized for the young people, many would leave for the towns, the farm management hit on the idea of forming an ensemble. The Iskra ensemble has appeared on television and had many successful tours to other countries. Now the farm receives a thousand letters a year requesting work there.

Professional workers in the arts are organized into unions. The Writers' Union, for instance, has a membership of over 8,000 writers and critics. There are several actors' unions, including the All-Russian Theater Association. Cinematographers, artists, composers and architects similarly have unions of their own.

Membership in a union is, of course, purely voluntary, but union membership does offer distinct advantages. Functioning as agents, for instance, artists' and writers' unions seek commissions for their members, negotiate contracts and arrange publication. Acting as public relations firms, they prepare articles about their members for newspapers and magazines, publish members' work in their own union journals and arrange for radio interviews and television appearances. If an artist or architect is working on a long-term project, his union can provide a loan to tide him over until his work is completed. (If the project is of scholarly or artistic importance, but of doubtful commercial interest, the loan may not have to be repaid.)

Unions also provide their members with such amenities as soundproof practice rooms, art studios and country retreats either free of charge or at reduced rates. Union publications are quite lively. Professional debates held at union clubs may be continued in the union's magazine or newspaper. The circulation of the Writers' Union *Literaturnaya Gazeta* is 2.5 million, and that of the Artists' Union, over 420,000.

A strong relationship exists between the Soviet Union's professional artists and
writers and its amateur groups. For example, more than 15,000 professional

composers, poets, actors and directors give their assistance to amateur stage and film groups. Theater and music directors eagerly scout for talent at amateur performances, and a significant proportion of those who eventually become professionals enter art, drama and music institutes through the door of amateur companies. The Cinematographers' Union provides young directors with a chance to start work through an experimental association called The Debut, and pays for the performances whether or not they are a commercial success. Similarly, the Artists' Union provides studios to young artists, and also pays for work/travel within the country. Experience has already shown that the rich impressions gained on such trips will sooner or later show up in finished canvases and pieces of sculpture.

Amateur choral groups, like this one performing at a Russian folk festival in the Kostroma region, provide a training ground for future professionals.

215

Any popular festival in the Soviet Union is bound to include folk dancing, and the themes of folk dancing inspire professional Soviet dance troupes as well. Folk dances, most of them carefully handed down over many generations, reveal the interests of the nationalities that devised them. Hunting peoples, for example, display in their unique choreography the habits of beasts and birds. Military valor is portrayed in the fast, gay dances of the Georgians and in the dashing ones of the Cossacks.

Modern Soviet choreographers remain faithful to folk themes and folklore in their own versions of traditional dancing. Their efforts are often a service to preservation. Before the Rossiya Troupe collected a repertoire of the many native dances of the Russian Federation, this largest of all the Soviet republics enjoyed only a few of its indigenous dances—Tatar, Daghestan and Ossetian. Now Rossiya represents the folk dances of the Russian Federation in all their variety.

Soviet choreographers from Igor Moiseyev to the young organizers of brand-new dance ensembles are following this same approach. The Folk Dance Ensemble of the USSR, one of our oldest troupes, has been is existence for over 40 years. It was founded in 1937 by Igor Moiseyev, originally a soloist and ballet master for the Bolshoi. Moiseyev's troupe performs dances based not only on the traditional folk dances of the many peoples of the Soviet Union, but also on folk dances from many other parts of the world. It has become, in fact, a tradition to prepare a popular dance from each country visited while on tour. When the troupe first visited the United States in 1958, members were pleased that the visit gave them an opportunity to learn still another foreign dance—the Virginia reel.

Whirl of the folk dance

Professional folk dance troups derive their choreography from traditional dances still performed all over the Soviet Union: (opposite page, top) a Byelorussian dance, (opposite page, bottom) a Georgian dance. (Right) Estonians dance at a folk festival and a Ukrainian dance (below) is performed by the Virsky Ensemble. Even when the dancers themselves do not form a circle, the circular pattern is maintained by the bystanders who, clapping and stamping in time to the music, become part of the dance themselves.

Though our folk art developed in the context of the utilitarian needs of every-day life, the lively variety of its shapes, astonishing workmanship and sheer artistic beauty have promoted it from mere handicraft to the level of fine art.

Whatever its humble origin, folk art is now considered fine enough for museums. A few years ago, a museum of folk art was set up in the ancient Russian town of Suzdal, about 150 miles northwest of Moscow. Here exhibits of decorative and applied art have proved especially popular with visitors and foreign tourists. But even these displays can give little idea of the enormous range of handicrafts produced here both in the past and today.

More than 200 handicrafts are practiced in the Russian Federation alone. These include lacquer work from the villages of Palekh, Mstera and Fedoskino;

delicate porcelain from Dmitrov and Dulevo; intricate woodwork produced by the Mari people; bone carvings from the Arctic North; Mordovian and Chuvash embroidery; woolen kerchiefs from the town of Pavlovo-Posad; linens from the Smolensk region, and articles made of birch bark and wood from Arkhangelsk and Yakutia.

Dolls and other toys, all created from wood with axe, saw, and chisel, are the specialty of the villages near Zagorsk. Zagorsk is, however, best known for its famous matrioshka, or Russian nesting dolls. Since they were first displayed at the World Exhibition in Paris in 1900, matrioshkas have changed styles many times. Today you can see matrioshkas holding bunches of flowers, baskets or sheaves of straw, whereas originally they were empty-handed.

Folk arts and artisans

(Left) *Folk architecture, so impressively presented at the Museum of Russian Wooden Architecture in the Suzdal Kremlin, is not confined to churches, as can be seen in two examples of fanciful window treatment (below). Both are located in European Russia.*

(Opposite page) *Although wood is a typical material, folk architecture is also expressed in stone, as in the pure form of the Pokrov Church on the Nerl River. To preserve such treasures craftsmen are still trained in the intricate, demanding skills used by the workers who originally created such buildings.*

Grassroots architecture

The restoration of architecture, paintings, sculpture, drawings, rare books and miniatures has become a separate branch of Soviet culture. The Ministry of Culture has 900 restoration experts, and as the meaning of restoration extends to include broad preservation methods, the All-Union Scientific Research Institute of Restoration has set scientists to work on problems of climate, stabilization of materials, transportation and packing technology, and bacterial or fungal damage.

The Assumption Cathedral in the Moscow Kremlin bore, by the 20th century, the scars of 4 centuries of weather as well as numerous invasions by man. Beneath the superficial damage were more ominous structural deficiencies.

To fortify the cathedral's foundations, cement mortar was pumped into the ground under pressure, while the walls were bound with steel ropes so workmen could replace the crumbling stones. Working at a formidable height on the domed roof, experts began the task of restoring and perfectly adjusting the positions of 2,000 sheets of red gold. Each

Heritage restored

was treated individually; some could be cleansed with chemical solutions; the most weatherbeaten ones were restored with a new coat of gold.

Inside the cathedral, frescoes originally decorating the north facade had entirely disappeared. Researchers were able to reproduce them from drawings discovered in an ancient book, and restorers com-

pleted every detail of the job using the techniques, both artistic and technical, of medieval masters.

This same extraordinary carefulness, both in research and in execution, has restored many of our most precious monuments—including the Moscow Kremlin—and works of art so that people may again enjoy them.

(Opposite page) The Cathedral of the Annunciation and the Facets Palace are both within the Moscow Kremlin. They, like other examples of our architectural heritage, require constant care to preserve the buildings and priceless interior art such as the frescoes (above) that adorn the rooms of the Facets Palace.

223

Much of the finest architecture of the Soviet Union was destroyed during the Second World War. The elegant Catherine Palace was among the casualties. (Left, and below) Its damaged façade and gutted interior are shown as they looked in 1944. (Below right) Painstaking work has restored the grand staircase, as well as the rest of the palace, to its former magnificence.

Today it is hard to believe the Catherine Palace was ever damaged, so perfect has been its reconstruction. (Below) To replace the exquisite parquetry floors, rare woods exactly duplicating the original choices were imported from many parts of the world.

Construction workers all over the Soviet Union receive instructions to stop work and summon archaeologists if they come across some unusual object. And this frequently happens. While repairing a mountain road in Armenia, builders discovered several half-buried caves. The archaeologists they called found a whole underground town complete with a church, burial vault and an inn. Priceless treasures were unearthed: a 3,000-year-old statuette, gold ornaments, an 11th-century bronze belt.

When people building roads, factories, tunnels or subways make such finds, the objects usually become new exhibits for regional museums. More than 500 museums in the Union Republics have departments of archaeology. Their collections are constantly being enriched with articles found by local inhabitants, and by their own staff.

The USSR organizes about 70 professional archaeological expeditions every year to promising areas such as the North Caucasus, Siberia, Central Russia, the Volga region and the island of Spitzbergen in the Arctic Ocean. Their finds too are usually exhibited in museums unless, like the primitive rock drawings recently found along the route of the Baikal-Amur Mainline, they are too large to move.

No matter what their actual worth, every piece in every local museum is considered priceless by the people of the area. When a farmer plowing the land or a construction worker excavating a road finds the merest coin or shard of pottery, it is a great event. Thus local museums are filled with ancient change and cooking utensils, stone implements, arrowheads, carvings and antique textiles. And when non-movable artifacts are found, travelers are enthusiastically encouraged to visit every one of them.

Archaeological treasures

(Opposite page, top) *Professionals work to unearth the remains of an ancient human burial in the Ukraine and (opposite page, bottom) of a baby mammoth preserved for many thousands of years in Siberian permafrost.*

Both central and regional museums display important pieces such as the carving of Medusa (right) found in the Ukraine and the "Gold Man" (left) found in Kazakhstan. The Gold Man is on exhibit in the Museum of Archaeology in Alma-Ata where staff archaeologists (below) work at cataloging pottery.

227

The collections in the Hermitage in Leningrad are an example of the broad range of art exhibited in major Soviet museums. (Left) Scythian gold articles were discovered during excavation of burial mounds in southern Ukraine. (Below) The grand architecture of the Hermitage makes an appropriate background for classical Greek and Roman sculpture. (Opposite page) In the Hall of Italian Art visitors to the Hermitage take in the magnificent paintings and sculpture as well as the grandeur of the hall itself.

Up to the time of the Revolution the broad masses of the people were unable to view and appreciate the masterpieces kept in the stately homes of the nobility and in the private collections of the rich. One of the early acts of the Revolution was to nationalize all major private collections so they would become equally accessible to all the people.

The leaders of the new state set themselves the task of introducing millions of uneducated workers and peasants to art. It was not an easy task, but the efforts have borne fruit. Today we can speak of a "museum boom" in the Soviet Union because not only the most famous but also less well-known halls are crowded with visitors. The Hermitage alone receives 4 million visitors a year.

The Soviet Communist Party has always given cultural education prime importance. The Constitution obligates the state to collect, safeguard and exhibit cultural treasures for the moral and esthetic education of the people. Questions of cultural treasures are regulated by the 1976 Law of the Protection and Use of Historical and Cultural Treasures, and these regulations apply both to public bodies and to private citizens.

Works of art may belong to the state, to collective farms, trade unions and other public organizations. They may also be in the private possession of citizens. Disposal by sale or as a gift is permitted, provided that the Ministry of Culture, which is responsible for safeguarding art treasures, is notified. Export abroad, not only of art treasures but also of any antique object and all works of art, is allowed only with the permission of the Ministry of Culture.

Museumgoers' paradise

Art of the Tretyakov

(Opposite page) *The Tretyakov Art Gallery in Moscow is the country's biggest museum of Russian and Soviet paintings. Its collections range from the early 15th-century painting of Archangel Michael by Andrei Rublyov (above) to more modern canvases such as the 19th-century portrait of M. Lopukhina by Vladimir Borovikovsky (above right) and the even more recent portrait of I. Morozov by Valentin Serov (below, right). Before the Revolution, such masterpieces were seldom available to the public.*

231

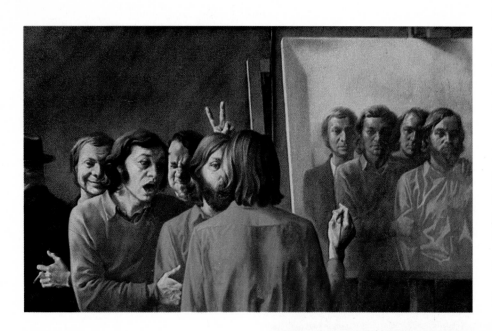

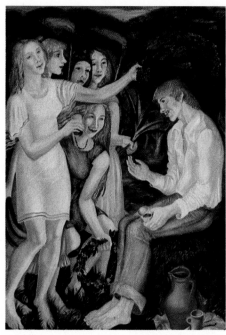

Contemporary Soviet art shows many styles.
The examples here are: (above)
"My Friends" by Alexander Petrov; (above right)
"The Ivan Kupala Festival," part of a triptych
by Natalya Pashukova; and (right)
"Wounded Rooster" by Alexander Sitnikov.
These paintings are all considered within
a humanist tradition directed to the masses
rather than to the elite.

Socialist realism, the main thrust in Soviet art today, was conceived by Maxim Gorky as art in the service of health and longevity, a celebration of the great happiness of living on earth. It inherits the best humanistic traditions of art in preceding ages and combines them with a new life-asserting esthetic.

Because Soviet art does not keep itself exclusive, but addresses itself to the masses, the best paintings—or simply "sensational" works—are discussed not only by narrow circles of esthetes but by millions of people who know and appreciate fine art. Books on art, including expensive art albums reproducing famous paintings, are sold out in no time. Newly built towns and cities are quick to open their own picture galleries. Severobaikalsk, a town that has just appeared on the map, already has a permanent exhibition hall.

A large number of works of art in the Soviet Union are commissioned by the Soviet state and by unions, factories or other people's organizations. This may seem strange to many. Yet when we look at ancient Greek statues or the paintings of the Renaissance masters, the idea that these wonderful creations are something less than art just because they were commissioned seems absurd. Indeed, Leonardo da Vinci, Raphael, Titian and hundreds of their gifted colleagues were commissioned to sculpt and paint by emperors, warlords, consuls, popes and cardinals. The great Picasso painted his "Guernica" on commission from the republican government of Spain.

Nonunion artists in the Soviet Union can and do make a living by working at publishing houses or painting as free-lancers. Most paintings, however, are commissioned for the approximately 5,000 exhibitions held each year in the USSR, and such commissions are provided to artists through their unions. The Soviet state, acting through the Ministry of Culture, may, for example, commission an artist to paint a picture that would best appeal to his artistic taste, and set a tentative price on the painting.

If the artist accepts the offer, he signs a contract and receives part of the money in advance. After the work is finished and is accepted by the exhibition board, the artist is paid either the balance of the money he is entitled to or a sum that may even exceed the amount stipulated in the contract. If the board rejects his work (which might also happen), the artist still keeps the sum of money he was paid in advance.

This system gives Soviet artists a chance to do the kind of work they like and to have a steady supply of orders. And, of course, nobody can stop them from painting pictures on their own—and selling them to anyone who wishes to buy—without signing any formal contracts.

Though socialist realism is the "mass" esthetic in Soviet art and the one we consider most uplifting, it is not the only one. Works of modernism, primitivism and impressionism are displayed in exhibition halls in Moscow, and lovers of today's avant garde art can readily buy such paintings in the USSR.

Today's artists

According to UNESCO statistics, the Soviet Union holds first place in the world, not only for the number of book titles published, but also for the number of readers. Muscovites alone buy up to 400,000 books a day, and everywhere new books sell out immediately.

It is hard even to describe the Soviet people's love of poetry. The smallest poetry edition is at least 15,000 copies, and the most popular poets—Yevtushenko, for example—are published in editions of 150,000 copies. Practically every family considers its home library the pride of the house. The reading public constantly discuss and argue about the books they have just read.

In this "land of most avid readers" there is great variety to choose from. The complex world of man's inner experience—his moral nature, love and obligations—are central themes of some outstanding works, but we also have our share of romantic novels, war literature and psychological thrillers. Lately there has been a remarkable outburst of "documentalism"—nonfiction works such as historical studies, travel notes, reflections, essays and personal journals.

The growing demand for books has boosted book printing to the point that an average of 4 million volumes comes off the printing presses every day, published in 89 languages by more than 200 publishing houses. In all, 80,000 titles a year are published in the USSR. Publishing houses specialize in such fields as fiction, science and political literature. Apart from the central or all-union publishing houses in Moscow and Leningrad there are ones in each Union Republic that publish literature in local languages.

Every year, 60-odd Soviet publishing houses publish more than 3,000 titles for children, or almost 500 million books. In spite of this number, children's publishing houses do not show a profit because children's books are sold at very low prices. A child's textbook that might sell for 5 rubles if it were for adults costs only 25 kopecks, and storybooks too sell for only a quarter the price of adult books of the same size and thickness. Three years ago, an ambitious project, the 50-volume Library of World Literature for Children, began to appear, and during the International Year of the Child one publishing house alone, Detskaya Literatura, produced 100 million children's books. The Malysh Publishing House produces books made as toys and folding books for the youngest children, fairy tales for preschool children to start them off reading and classics for older children. It is now putting out an attractive series about traffic rules, the usefulness of physical exercises in the morning and the need for a careful attitude toward nature.

Foreign classical works considered appropriate for publication in the USSR are printed in numbers far exceeding their total printing in their native countries. To cite but a few examples, over 31 million copies of works by Jack London have been printed in the Soviet Union, and 21 million copies of works by Mark Twain. American literature ranks first in the number of translations made in the USSR—779 titles within 2 years—and every third book published in the Soviet Union is by a foreign author. Editions range from 50,000 to 150,000 copies per title.

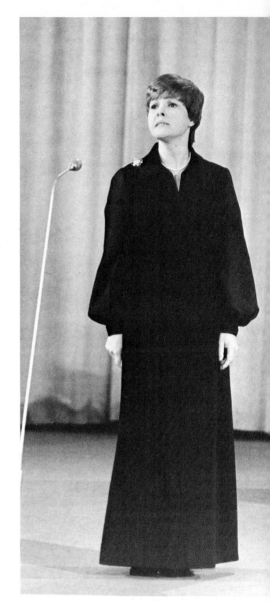

Poet Bella Akhmadulina recites her own verse at a poetry reading. Poetry readings draw large audiences, and even within the home poetry is often recited as a family entertainment.

234

Books by the million

Grigori Khodzher, the Nanain writer, is a source of great pride to his people. Only decades ago, few Nanains were literate.

Yuri Trifonov is a novelist and short-story writer who acknowledges an affinity with Hemingway, Faulkner and Updike.

Valentin Rasputin, one of the most popular writers in the USSR, lives and works in Siberia, the land of his birth.

New foreign novels are often published in magazines, and news of their publication spreads immediately. One could say there has been a "Year of Kurt Vonnegut" or a "Year of Arthur Hailey." *Ragtime* by E. L. Doctorow was very popular here, and so was *The Summer Before Dark* by Doris Lessing. Second only to American books is French and British literature, followed by the work of the Federal Republic of Germany, Japan and the socialist countries.

Writers can work free from the responsibilities of everyday life at writers' work homes like this one in Peredelkino, near Moscow.

The popularity of newspapers and magazines in the USSR has not been affected by television and radio, even though they are natural competitors. Circulation grows steadily each year, limited only by a noticeable paper shortage.

The total circulation of the Soviet Union's 7,923 newspapers is 170 million copies. This means there are 659 copies for every thousand people (and many of these are children too young to read the newspaper). The leading paper is *Pravda*, the organ of the Communist Party Central Committee (10.6 million copies), followed by *Komsomolskaya Pravda*, published by the Young Communist League (9.9 million copies). *Izvestia*, a government paper, and *Trud*, the central trade union paper, each have a circulation of about 8 million. Library copies of the Soviet sports newspaper, *Sovetski Sport*, are read until holes appear in them.

To make printed information available to the various peoples of the USSR, newspapers in Union Republics, autonomous republics and autonomous regions are published in the language of the indigenous populations of those regions and also in Russian.

Soviet newspapers are usually from 4 to 8 pages. Despite their small size they are packed with information and commentary on domestic and international developments selected for their pertinence to matters of moment. The major newspapers carry no advertisements. News on consumer goods appears in weekly advertisement supplements, and advertisements do appear in local papers.

Magazines and periodicals are also in high demand. They range from the weekly satirical *Krokodil* and the children's monthly *Murzilka* to publications that cover such subjects as health, agri-

Spreading the news

culture, economics, history, science and youth concerns. *Kommunist,* the theoretical journal of the Communist Party Central Committee, has a circulation of a million.

Literary journals play an important role in the Soviet Union. Most new works of Soviet fiction are first published in these journals, and *Inostrannaya Literature* (Foreign Literature) is a window on foreign prose and poetry.

Most popular of all are the women's magazines, *Rabotnitsa* and *Krestyanka.* Despite the fact that these magazines have circulations of, respectively, 13 and 6.5 million, they are almost always in short supply at newsstands and kiosks because of the paper shortage. That is why most people prefer to receive magazines by subscription. Both these magazines cover a wide range of interests for working women. Almost half the people

engaged in industry are women, so *Rabotnitsa* prints frequent interviews with management and trade union representatives and with doctors regarding working conditions for women (particularly expectant mothers). *Krestyanka* concerns itself with rural problems. Politics, the arts and literature are covered in both magazines, but pride of place is taken by the eternal themes of love, marriage and the family, children, fashions and cooking. 237

(Left) *The Ostankino TV Tower in Moscow is a major broadcasting center. The combined height of the tower and aerial is 533 meters.* (Below) *A television musical is being filmed in one of the studios within the center. Programing originating at Ostankino and other centers is broadcast nationwide at convenient local times.*

(Opposite page) *Television relay stations form a network that reaches even the most outlying areas of the Soviet Union. This one is in Kamchatka where dog sleds and contemporary technology exist side by side.*

The Soviet Union's television network brings a wide range of programs to more than 80 percent of its population. To transmit to remote areas, programs are relayed by the Orbita system of ground stations and by satellite. Practically all programs are transmitted in color.

Most popular of the programs originating at the Central TV Station in Moscow is "Vremya" (Time). "Vremya" presents the major news of the day, including political commentary on foreign and domestic affairs, reports from foreign correspondents, economic, scientific and cultural news, and the day's sports. "Vremya" is aired at 9 o'clock each evening (and repeated at convenient local times across the breadth of Siberia and the Far East).

The Central TV Station's daily broadcasts reflect people's major interests: popular science, health, sports, travel and music. Besides such programs as "Good Night, Little Ones" and "In Fairy Tale Land," children see many cartoons. Local TV stations in cities all across the country air some of these programs and also originate programs of their own.

Film and television

Annual movie attendance in the USSR is 4 billion, a figure that attests to both the popularity and the accessibility of films. There are cinemas in almost every town; besides permanent movie houses, mobile projectors make it possible to show films to farm workers in the fields, construction workers in the taiga forests, and herders high in the mountains.

Soviet films depict contemporary life, and they tend to raise complex moral questions. The Soviet people also remain interested in the classics of the 50's and 60's; these still circulate widely among the country's 150,000 permanent and mobile cinemas. Soviet film makers have worked on a number of joint productions with colleagues from abroad, and many of these films have proved popular with moviegoers. A Soviet-American documentary, "The Unknown War," a 20-part film shown on American television and at the Kennedy Center for the Performing Arts in 1977-78, was awarded the Grand Prix at the New York International Film Festival and the main prize at the Miami Documentary Film Festival.

The popularity of the puppet theater is as great as ever with children such as those (left) watching a performance at the Moscow Puppet Theater. Puppet shows are also scheduled for adults. (Below, left) Each republic has its own puppet theater; this one is in Kirgizia. (Below, right) After the show young spectators may be allowed to visit the puppet masters and their puppets.

(Opposite page, right) The acknowledged master of masters is Sergei Obraztsov, director of the State Central Puppet Theater in Moscow. (Opposite page, left) The scene shown is from Obraztsov's production "Noah's Ark."

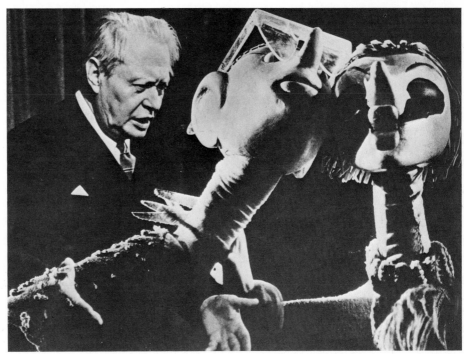

Perhaps no form of public entertainment has such deep popular roots as our puppet theater. The date of the actual beginning of the puppet theater in Russia is unknown, but puppet shows at the court of Ivan the Terrible in the mid-16th century are documented. Certainly puppeteers roamed the towns and villages of Old Russia during the last century. They set up their booths at crowded fairs and markets, and to the sound of a hurdy-gurdy, ginger-headed Petrushka skillfully bested his enemies—the merchant, the landowner and the policeman. Then, as now, the success of a puppet show hinged on its keen satire, sparkling humor and topicality—a boldness that often led the authorities of Old Russia to persecute itinerant puppeteers.

Following the October Revolution, the puppet theater advanced rapidly. The first state-sponsored puppet theaters were established in the mid-20's, and now there are 120 puppet theaters staffed by professional producers, artists and actors.

All 3 of the basic puppet types are in use—marionettes operated by strings, hand puppets and puppets operated by rods. When puppeteers are handling very large puppets, they appear on the stage along with the "actors."

The Central Puppet Theater in Moscow, better known as the Obraztsov Puppet Theater after the name of its founder and director, opened in 1931. It gives at least 2 performances daily, one of which is always for adults who never fail to be amused at puppet satires that poke fun at profiteers caught in their own greed, at the comic results of mismanagement, at the foibles of prejudice or the struggle between good and evil.

241

World of the puppet

Circus in a single ring

Soviet circuses, performed in a single ring, feature a stunning array of acrobats, jugglers, trapeze artists and clowns. Most unusual are acts (opposite page) that use exotic animals, unlikely combinations such as the horse and tiger act at the Moscow Circus (left) and Yuri Kuklachev's performing cats (right). (Below) The fiery Ossetian riders are a rousing favorite.

It is as difficult to get a ticket to a concert given by a famous symphony orchestra in the Soviet Union as it is to get a ticket to a rock group. This does not mean that everyone prefers classical music; quite the opposite, there are still more people who prefer light music. But through esthetic education beginning in childhood, the masses are gradually improving their cultural standards to the point where today the state can support more than 100 symphony orchestras.

There are still too few performances and not enough space for the growing number of music lovers. The Ministry of Culture does the best it can to be fair to all under these circumstances. It reserves blocks of tickets for tourist groups, for foreign visitors and for various organizations that have expressed interest in a particular performance their members wish to see. Still there are always lines of people at box offices waiting to buy tickets to each performance, as well as crowds of hopefuls in front of the hall seeking to buy a ticket someone else cannot use that night. And, as everywhere, there are those who are lucky enough to have a friend in the box office and manage to get tickets when no one else can. There is no doubt the growing popularity of music has also created inconveniences for music lovers.

Our tastes in symphony music are diverse. Of course Bach, Beethoven, Mozart, Tchaikovsky, Mussorgsky and Rachmaninov never "get old." Soviet composers such as Prokofiev, Shostakovich and Aram Khachaturyan have long since become classics. Among our concertgoers, however, a love of the classics does not preclude interest in the more recent and innovative works of both Soviet and foreign composers.

Although Moscow and Leningrad are the most important music centers, other cities try not to lag behind. Recent years have seen a certain progress toward raising performance standards. Today one can enjoy concerts by symphony orchestras at the philharmonic societies in virtually all our large cities. These societies are self-sufficient organizations, but should box office returns fail to cover expenses, subsidies are provided by the state to pay the musicians in full.

Amateur groups are a basic feature of musical life in the Soviet Union. It is estimated that, taking into account every sort of amateur musical group, there are about 15 million nonprofessional musicians in the country.

Palaces of Culture often have their own ensembles made up of students, farmers, workers, engineers, teachers or doctors who may perform anything from folk songs or the work of local composers to difficult classic symphonies.

Light music—pop, rock and jazz— evokes many disapproving remarks among Soviet critics. Briefly their comments can be summed up in one phrase: there are many performers, but few personalities. This criticism seems to be justified, although there are some stars.

The Soviet Union's favorite pop singers are of various backgrounds and pursue various styles, from the traditions of the chanteuse to the increasingly popular sounds (at least with the young) of rock and jazz. Alla Pugacheva, whose records have sold over 100 million copies, only sings about things that are close to her heart. Each of Alla's songs is a performance in itself, a 3-minute comedy, lyrical drama or tragedy starring herself suffering, rejoicing, joking, weeping.

Another very popular singer, Edita Piecha, grew up in Poland but later became attached to the tenderness, lyricism and sincerity of Russian folk songs.

David Tukhmanov, whose own rock compositions have been hit songs since the 1960's, feels that "the patriotic theme is the mainstream of my work. I write songs about the beauty of work, comradeship, honesty and friendship. The modern beats I use make the songs more energetic." Another rock star, Alexander Gradsky, is working on a rock opera called "A Stadium." The work is dedicated to the tragic events in Chile during the coup of 1973.

(Opposite page) *The magnificence of the Philharmonic Society Concert Hall in Tbilisi gives some idea of the ambitiousness of the Soviet state's move to bring the finest music to all its citizens.*

(Below) *Leonid Kogan, virtuoso violinist, is a soloist with the Moscow Philharmonic and winner of the Lenin Prize.*

Pop, rock and classical

Theater and opera in the Soviet Union entirely lack what can be described as a commercial approach. They are expected to satisfy people's cultural needs, to enrich their minds and hearts. The government meets this obligation by not stinting on financing.

Five years ago, the Vilnius Opera and Ballet theater moved into a new building that cost 12.5 million rubles. A new opera production there costs as much as 50,000 rubles. Yet the tickets are not expensive: only a ruble to 2.5 rubles for an evening performance. (Even at the Bolshoi tickets range from 90 kopecks to only 3 rubles.) The Vilnius Theater's annual receipts amount to 500,000 rubles, while its annual expenses are 1.7 million; to make up the difference, revenues are supplemented by Lithuania's state budget.

The art of the Russian drama theater is exemplified primarily by the Maly Theater and the Moscow Art Theater whose repertoires are rooted in the rich traditions of the Russian stage. However, Moscow alone has 30 theaters representing different trends in theatrical art. The foreign visitor is generally interested to see the Russian classics—works by Gogol, Turgenev, Dostoyevsky and Chekhov—but it is just as interesting to see how Molière or Shakespeare are interpreted on the Russian stage. There is also the choice of more modern playwrights such as Tennessee Williams, Heinrich Böll and Robert Bolt, or Soviet writers such as Aruzov, Rozov and Vampilov. Modern Soviet dramas dealing with moral and ethical questions are most successful.

An evening at the theater

Classic theater and opera, represented in scenes from: (opposite page) Anton Chekhov's *The Cherry Orchard*, (below, top) Shakespeare's *Richard III*, (below, bottom) Rossini's comic opera *La Cambiale di Matrimonia*. (Right) Rimsky-Korsakov's opera *Sadko* gives set and costume designers a grand opportunity to display their talents.

(Overleaf) Rimsky-Korsakov's *Sadko* as performed at the Bolshoi in Moscow

The classic school of dancing is the basis of all our ballet productions, but our newer choreographers are beginning to favor a bold, innovative handling of traditional dance. Audiences in the Soviet Union are no longer easy to impress. Beauty and virtuosity alone are not enough, nor are artists satisfied with restrictive classicism. People now want more "intellectual" ballet, productions that leave them with something to think about. The number of new artists—dancers, composers, choreographers—rising to prominence in response to this new development in public taste is a sign that a qualitatively new stage in the development of Soviet ballet is about to begin.

Certainly Aram Khachaturyan's "Spartacus," choreographed by Yuri Grigorovich; Rodion Shchedrin's "Seagull" by Maya Plisetskaya; Kirill Molchanov's "Macbeth" by Vladimir Vasilyev, and Andrei Petrov's "Creation of the World" by Valentin Yelizaryev have been justly acclaimed as being in a class of their own.

Dancers, composers and choreographers alike are able to respond to people's needs because the state has brought their art within the reach of the general public. Not only do leading companies go on tour to different parts of the country, but also the state has established traveling ballet troupes. Two outstanding traveling troupes are the Moscow Suvenir and the Leningrad Ballet Ensemble. Through the language of dance, the directors of these 2 companies respond to the concerns with love, success and failure, or relations between the generations which preoccupy young people. The dancing is more spontaneous, less committed to tradition; their productions verge on improvisation. Sometimes, in fact, classic dance in these companies is combined with variety-show dancing and with elements of sport. The result can truly be called "modern style."

The notion of "provincial ballet" no longer exists in the USSR. Dancers for ballet companies receive their training at 19 schools, and prizes at Soviet and at international ballet competitions have been won by graduates from ballet schools not only in Moscow, Leningrad, Kiev and Riga, but also in Perm, Yerevan, Novosibirsk, Voronezh and Alma-Ata. Talented children may go to any of these ballet schools as well as the most famous schools of all, at Leningrad and Moscow. Like pupils in ordinary schools, they study general subjects. In addition, they learn French (since ballet terminology is in that language) and have ballet classes every day. Regardless of which school children attend, their education for dance is under the guidance of highly experienced teachers from the Leningrad or Moscow schools.

Children begin their specialized training at these ballet schools at the age of 10. In the Leningrad school, there are typically 600 applications for the 60 places offered. Accompanied by mothers or grandmothers, the girls and boys take part in 3 elimination rounds. Only the most gifted become pupils at the Leningrad Ballet School.

As in America, ballet students start their performing career in the children's episodes of the "Nutcracker Suite" and "Sleeping Beauty," as well as in school productions specially choreographed for children.

(Below) *Members of the Bolshoi in leotards and warm-up suits keep in practice between rehearsals and performances. Most of these men and women have studied dance since the age of 10 or younger.*

(Opposite page) *Maya Plisetskaya performs the title role in Anna Karenina. Plisetskaya typifies the purity and grace of the classic style still overwhelmingly preferred in the USSR.*

Ballet and beyond

(Opposite page) *Nadezhda Pavlova and Vyacheslav Gordeyev perform in Tchaikovsky's The Nutcracker.* (Below) *Valeri Anisimov dances in the ballet Chopiniana at the Bolshoi and* (right) *a scene from the Shakuntala to music by Sergei Balasanyan is performed at the Stanislavsky and Nemirovich-Danchenko Academic Music Theater in Moscow.*

253

"The Russians mix politics with sports!" one often reads in the Western press. Yes, we do, but not in the sense Western writers mean. To us sports are not a political trump card, but an effective means of strengthening understanding, peace and friendship between nations. We see sports as an opportunity for broad international contacts at a popular level, a level where the warmth of human relationships proves more important and more lasting than the excitement surrounding competitions.

We are proud of our athletes, just as fans in any other country are, but we do not seek to make political capital out of their achievements. Many foreign visitors have noted that Soviet fans are amazingly objective. They applaud enthusiastically "the football wizards" from Brazil, the intrepid Canadian pucksters and the formidable judo wrestlers from Japan. A great deal has been said and written here in admiration of Eric Heiden, the phenomenal American speed skater.

The Soviet state has always shown concern for the health of its citizens, and sports are essential to a healthy nation. Therefore, sports are to us a subject of domestic social policy. The aim of this policy is to ensure that our youths grow up agile and strong in body and mind, that middle-aged people do not suffer from illnesses caused by insufficient exercise, that old people do not waste time in the corridors of hospitals and, lastly, that an effective all-out struggle be waged against drinking and smoking.

The right to rest and leisure, proclaimed in Article 41 of the Constitution of the USSR, envisages the development of sport and physical culture on a mass scale. Measures taken to promote sports include legal rulings. It is now a rule, for example, that every new city neighborhood for 30,000 to 50,000 residents must have its own stadium, gymnasium and swimming pool.

Implementation of Soviet sports policy involves considerable expense. But the sizable expenditure means that our sports enthusiasts have at their disposal over 3,000 large stadiums, nearly 71,000 gymnasiums, 106,000 soccer fields, and 394,000 volleyball, basketball and tennis courts.

Sports are organized for top athletes by sport clubs sponsored by nationwide organizations such as trade unions and the military. Sport club teams, equivalent in skill to professional teams elsewhere, attract talent from all over the country and compete with one another. Team members, however, are not paid athletes, and all continue to work at their usual occupations in spite of the heavy demands of sport. Each team—the Spartak soccer and ice hockey teams or the Torpedo soccer team—has its fans, and games between such rivals draw large crowds of wildly enthusiastic spectators.

Sports on a mass scale are organized by the voluntary sports societies (DSO's) in every sort of enterprise from repair shops and banks to collective farms and factories. DSO's have a membership of more than 60 million sports enthusiasts who are entitled to the free use of stadiums, gyms, pools, courts and playing 255

Sports spectacular

fields, as well as sports equipment and gear. Yet member athletes pay only a token membership fee of 30 kopecks a year.

Children are introduced to physical culture from an early age. At kindergartens the day starts with morning exercises. Throughout the 10 years of school, physical education is a compulsory subject and as much a requirement for graduation as mathematics or literature.

If a child has weak health or a physical disability, he or she receives special care in physical education. Children in perfect health, on the other hand, may go out for sports offered outside the regular physical education program. Children may join a sports group at school or at a Young Pioneers' Palace or one run by a DSO in the neighborhood.

Junior sports schools are the highest level of juvenile sports. Compared with sports sections, they have better instructors and equipment, and the training is more intensive. Most specialize in one particular sport, such as gymnastics or soccer, with a view to preparing children for serious competition. Children attend most junior sports schools after classes, but some are general schools as well.

Kolya Zholus, 2 years old, and his baby sister, Nadya, prepare to take a swim at the Moskva swimming pool in Moscow.

Although there are nearly 6,000 junior sports schools attended by almost 2 million youngsters, it is often difficult to get into one. Since the instructors are responsible for a new generation of star athletes, the success of their work is judged by how well their students perform. Children who do not show promise are not accepted for training. This is, perhaps, a wrong practice. The matter is widely discussed in our press and much criticism is leveled at officials responsible for children's physical education (school principals, the sports committee of an area's Department of Education, even the Sports Committee of a republic or the USSR government itself).

While the matter is being settled, ordinary citizens who are sports enthusiasts are attempting to rectify the situation by organizing neighborhood sports activities. This movement is growing in scale, promoted by local soviets and various sports organizations.

For soccer, ice hockey, and model airplane flying we have a competitive system that begins at the level of children's "backyard" teams. Backyard teams are made up of neighborhood boys, and any boy who wishes to join may try out for the team. The boys themselves choose the best players for the team and also manage their own teams. Competition starts with several backyard teams contesting the title of street champion. Street champion teams in turn compete for district championship, and so on at city, region and republic levels. These competitions, important enough to be shown on TV, are managed by such organizations as a city sports committee. Teams that need better equipment or transportation are subsidized. Volunteers—athletics teachers, for instance—search out financial help and also lend their coaching expertise. The final winning team receives a trophy presented by the players of the USSR national soccer or ice hockey team. While the competitions are in progress, scouts from junior sports schools and even from major sports clubs scout for young talent among the backyard players.

Juvenile sports do have problems: good sports equipment is often in short supply, and some schools do not give physical education proper attention. But the mass nature of our children's sports definitely outweighs its few difficulties.

Young people who continue into higher education continue their physical education as well. Besides a compulsory program during the first few years every university or institute offers a choice of sports groups, and most students go in for sports despite the fact that study, research and volunteer activities take up much of their time. Most of the Soviet Union's sports stars are college students. Although some are enrolled at physical culture institutes to prepare for careers in coaching, many others are mathematicians, journalists, doctors or historians. Sports stars train apart from other students at sports facilities shared by the USSR national team or the select team of a republic or DSO.

Not only students and athletes, but also people in every walk of life and of any age have the opportunity to take up sports if they wish to. At many factories and offices, a 15-minute break is scheduled in the middle of the day for what is called at-work gymnastics. Nearly 20 million people engage in this form of regular physical exercise. City and village stadiums are made available to all, including middle-aged people who attend physical fitness groups.

Occasionally, sports groups at industrial enterprises become first-rate teams. The Torpedo soccer team of the Likhachev auto works in Moscow has been in the top league for decades, winning the title of USSR Champion and the USSR Cup several times.

There are no sports stars among the employees of the Lenin-Komsomol auto works, but the plant is outstanding for the mass character of sports there. It offers its employees and their families a choice of 25 sports groups as well as a stadium with several soccer fields, basketball and tennis courts, an aquatics center, an indoor track and field arena and several gymnasiums. The plant is currently building an ice rink for its ice hockey players and figure skaters.

In the Soviet Union today, there are nearly 160,000 Masters of Sport—the highest rating in this country. We are proud of this, but we are even more proud of the mass nature of sports in the Soviet Union. And we are pleased with another fact: there are about 300,000 highly qualified specialists, paid and volunteer, working in the field of physical education. That means that the mass sports movement is developing on a scientific basis. Instructors and coaches are working for a healthy nation as effectively as medical personnel. Only their means are different.

Hundreds of thousands of sports enthusiasts turn out for the May Day sports parade in Red Square outside the walls of the Kremlin.

Children's participation in sports is encouraged by government policy and supported by various sports groups and volunteers. (Above) Boys in a sports school practice dribbling basketballs. (Left) Swimmers at a sports center learn from a doctor the effects of exercise on their own pulse rates.

(Opposite page, top) Young gymnasts have yet to achieve the grace that more practiced students display (opposite page, bottom right).

(Opposite page, bottom left) A hockey player wears full uniform and equipment supplied through one of many sports associations.

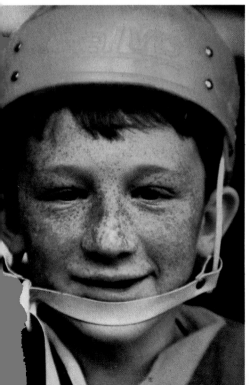

Spartakiads of the Peoples of the USSR are countrywide athletic competitions in which millions of athletes participate. Summer Spartakiads have been held every 4 years since 1956, Winter Spartakiads since 1966.

Competition to qualify for the finals begins 2 years before the games. The first-level Spartakiads are held by the sports clubs of factories, plants, offices, schools, farms and construction projects. Both beginners and champions compete. Winners at the first level compete at the second level for district, town, city, regional, territorial and Union Republic championships. Winners of the Union Republic Spartakiads form teams to enter the finals along with teams from the country's biggest sports centers, Moscow and Leningrad. Individual results, although unofficial, are also recorded, and may help a person be accepted into a major team.

Spartakiad national finals are traditionally held at Lenin Central Stadium in Moscow, the Soviet Union's largest sports complex. In addition to the more than 20 traditional Olympic sports, Spartakiads include a School Spartakiad (for children from 7 to 17 years old), competition in technical sports such as marksmanship, model airplane flying, wilderness skills and driving as well as games for rural sportsmen who have had less opportunity for training than others.

Spartakiad results are followed with keen interest. Many athletes who win in these games go on to distinguish themselves as world champions. Thus Vladimir Yashchenko first attracted attention by winning the high jump event at the National School Spartakiad and later went on to become world record holder in the high jump. Results also have a decisive influence on the composition of USSR

The Peoples' Games

(Opposite page) *Opening ceremonies at Spartakiad 1979 featured banners carried by* *members of sports societies and (this page) pictures formed by holding up colored cards.*

national teams for the Olympic Games.

Spartakiads prompt millions of people to pursue sports in a serious fashion. For instance, 87 million people took part in all stages of Spartakiad-79, and over 8,000 athletes made it to the finals. For the first time, Spartakiad-79 went beyond purely national competition. Besides Soviet athletes, competitors from 84 countries took part in the events. Twelve world records were set, evidence that Spartakiads are not only an example of the Soviet Union's mass approach to sports, but also have significance for international sports.

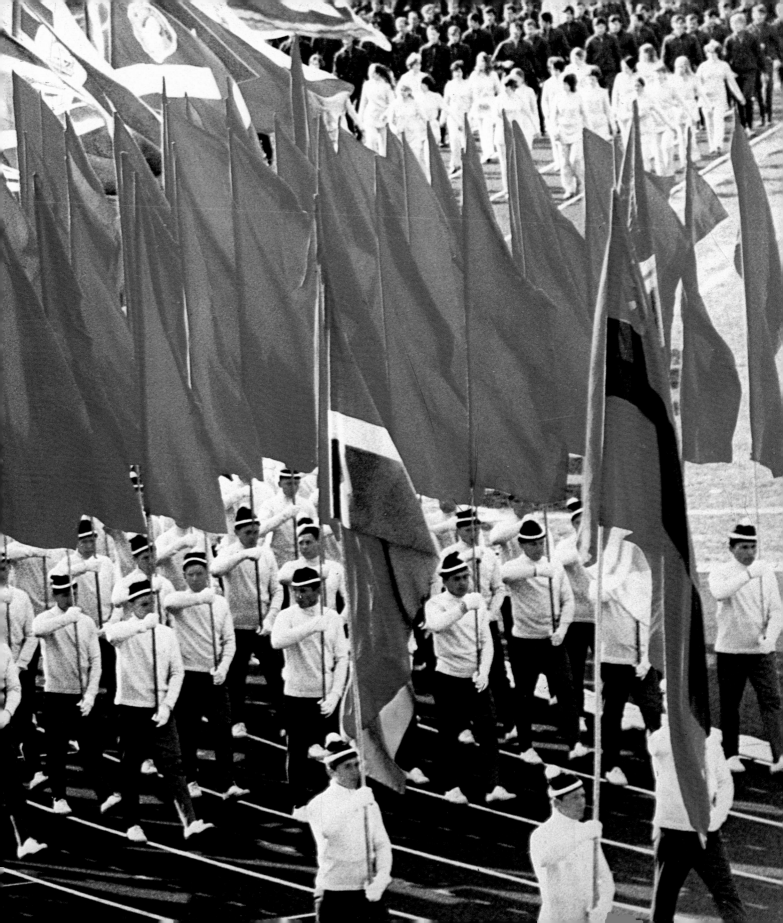

Olympiad-80 was an occasion for the USSR to build and renovate needed sports facilities in the Olympic cities of Moscow, Leningrad, Kiev, Tallinn and Minsk. The designers and planners did not seek to create sensational architecture; none of the structures are pretentious, but they will all still be in use many years after the games are over.

When Moscow was chosen for the Olympic Games, designers and builders speeded up work on plans already in existence. Of the total of 99 new or remodeled facilities required, 76 were in Moscow itself. The Big Sports Arena, part of the Lenin Central Stadium sports complex, was modernized.

The main arena seats 103,000 and was the site of the soccer finals and track-and-field events. Europe's biggest indoor stadium, with a seating capacity of 45,000, is located near the Mir Prospekt. An indoor swimming facility was built near the stadium, with separate pools for divers and swimmers. The stadium itself is fitted with a sliding partition so that it can be divided into equal halls. For the Olympics, the halls were used for boxing and basketball competitions, but at other times they are also used for indoor soccer games, Russian hockey matches (played with a ball rather than a puck), and track and field. Evening balls for young people, New Year celebrations for children, and variety shows and circuses are held there too.

A rowing canal in Krylatskoye on the outskirts of Moscow is brand-new, as is the indoor "fast" wooden cycling track nearby. Residents in the Izmailovo district received an all-purpose gymnasium and those in Luzhniki a hall for games, and a sports pavilion for soccer and track was built on Leningrad Prospekt.

Moscow also constructed new hotels, an Olympic press center (now used for Novosti Press Agency headquarters) and a new television center in Ostankino, in Moscow.

The Olympic Village in Moscow is a complex of 18 apartment houses, each 16 stories high, situated on generous grounds. Athletes and coaches lived in 1-, 2- and 3-room suites with all modern conveniences. The village provided facilities for training, leisure and rest. For training, there are 3 gymnasiums, 3 swimming pools, 3 soccer fields, and basketball and volleyball courts. These are already being used for competitions among residents of the neighborhood. The cultural center provides a concert hall, 2 cinemas, a discothèque, and a library with 10,000 volumes in many languages. Temporary chapels for religious worship were also provided. For the first time in the history of the Olympic Games, an entertainment program to ease pregame tensions was offered to the residents of Olympic Village.

Olympic Village was designed to be a complete city neighborhood. After a minor "face lift," 15,000 Muscovites moved into the apartments, where they enjoy the same sports facilities and culture center that Olympic athletes used during the games. Moscow is a large city, and the distances between hotels, stadiums and press center are considerable. To organize an efficient shuttle

Olympiad-80

service during Olympiad-80, the city allocated 7,200 buses and a fleet of 4,000 cars. Tourists also used the fast and efficient Moscow Metro and the new circumferential highway that was recently built as part of Moscow's accelerated city plan.

Tallinn, site of the Olympic regatta, benefited from new construction too. A marina with berths for 750 yachts and launches was built in the estuary of the Pirita River. The city built a concert hall and gymnasium, indoor dry-dock facilities and repair shops, a new sea passenger port and, of course, an Olympic Village now inhabited by Tallinn residents.

About 1.5 billion viewers watched the Olympiad-80 opening and closing ceremonies on television and enjoyed numerous special cultural programs as well. The games themselves were shown every day from early in the morning until late at night all over the Soviet Union. The cultural program for the Olympic Games included performances by the Moiseyev Dancers, the famous Pyatnitski Choir, the Moscow Art Theater and Taganka Theater, as well as individual star performers and festivals of national folk dance and music. These fine performances were relayed by television to Volgograd, Pskov, Novgorod, Yerevan, Tbilisi, Tashkent, Bokhara and Samarkand. Olympiad-80 gave the USSR an opportunity to welcome tourists from many nations and also to bring the excitement of sports and the enjoyment of culture to our own people.

Most of the major events of the 1980 Olympiad were held at Lenin Central Stadium in Luzhniki. Extensive renovation of the stadium included the installation of lighting for night use.

Index

(Numbers in italic refer to illustrations.)

273